Richa Tilokani is a marketing, communication, and advertising professional who enjoys writing books and poems and has contributed to myriad magazines, newspapers, blogs and anthologies.

Her first book, *The Teachings of Bhagavad Gita: Timeless Wisdom for the Modern Age,* was published in 2021 and nominated by the PragatiE Vichaar Literature Festival '22 in the Best Debut Non-Fiction category.

She holds a master's degree in Business Administration (MBA) from SP Jain Institute of Management & Research, Mumbai.

7 LESSONS of KARMA YOGA

Mindset Management for *Work–Life Success*

RICHA TILOKANI

Published by
Rupa Publications India Pvt. Ltd 2024
7/16, Ansari Road, Daryaganj
New Delhi 110002

Sales centres:
Bengaluru Chennai
Hyderabad Jaipur Kathmandu
Kolkata Mumbai Prayagraj

Copyright © Richa Tilokani 2024

The views and opinions expressed in this book are the
author's own and the facts are as reported by her which
have been verified to the extent possible, and the publishers
are not in any way liable for the same.

All rights reserved.
No part of this publication may be reproduced, transmitted,
or stored in a retrieval system, in any form or by any means,
electronic, mechanical, photocopying, recording or otherwise,
without the prior permission of the publisher.

P-ISBN: 978-93-6156-468-0
E-ISBN: 978-93-6156-880-0

First impression 2024

10 9 8 7 6 5 4 3 2 1

The moral right of the author has been asserted.

Printed in India

This book is sold subject to the condition that it shall not,
by way of trade or otherwise, be lent, resold, hired out, or otherwise
circulated, without the publisher's prior consent, in any form of
binding or cover other than that in which it is published.

To my family and friends

shri bhagavaan uvaacha
sannyasaḥ karma-yogash cha nihshreyasa-karaavubhau
tayos tu karma-sannyaasaat karma-yogo vishishyate

[The Supreme Lord said: both the paths of Karm Sanyas
(renunciation of actions) and Karm Yoga
(working in devotion) lead to the supreme goal,
but Karm Yoga is superior to Karm Sanyas.]

—Bhagavad Gita 5:2

Contents

Introduction: Karm Yoga—The Art of Work   xi

Mindset Management: Becoming a Karm Yogi

1. Understanding the Self: Mindset Management through the Three Gunas   3
2. Physical and Mental Wellness: Mindset Management with a Focus on Health   28
3. Understanding One's Role in Society: Compulsory Social Duties or Obligations   55

Leadership Lessons

4. Karm Yoga Leadership Lesson 1: Discharge All Duties   77
5. Karm Yoga Leadership Lesson 2: Duties Must Be Discharged with Advanced Intelligence   88
6. Karm Yoga Leadership Lesson 3: Duties Must Be Discharged within the Framework of Yogic Action, and Treated like Worship   98
7. Karm Yoga Leadership Lesson 4: Avoid Adharmic Actions, Increase Dharmic Actions   109
8. Karm Yoga Leadership Lesson 5: Increase Duties that Lead to Community Welfare   123
9. Karm Yoga Leadership Lesson 6: Do Not Work Only for the Fruits of the Action   138

10. Karm Yoga Leadership Lesson 7: Surrender the Ego, Do Not Think You Are the Doer 154

Conclusion: Karm Yoga in Action—Eternal Philosophy for the New Age 168

Acknowledgements 181

Introduction

Karm Yoga: The Art of Work

yogah karmasu kaushalam

[With yoga, we can excel in action.]

(Bhagavad Gita 2:50)

The word 'yoga' originates from the Sanskrit root *yuj*, which means 'to join'. It lends itself to multiple interpretations—the union with the self, the union of the self with the higher Self, the art of life, performing an action skilfully, and the principles of holistic wellness, amongst others. (It is surely not a series of laptops, as the Lenovo advertisement would have us believe.)

yogasthah kurukarmani sangam tyaktva dhananjaya
siddhya siddhyo samo bhutva samatvam yoga uchyate

(Bhagavad Gita 2:48)

The Gita states that yoga is performing one's duty without attachment to success or failure, with equanimity. Yoga is all this and so much more—an enriching, rewarding, and mystical journey that elevates, purifies, and transforms. When it fuses with the higher actions of life called *karm* or work, it elevates to Karm Yoga, the art of work.

Origin of Karm Yoga

The science of yoga was first mentioned in the Gita, one of the most sacred texts in the world.

> *imam vivasvate yogam proktavaan aham avyayam*
> *vivasvan manave praha manur iksvakave bravit*

(Bhagavad Gita 4:1)

Lord Krishna says here, 'I first shared it with the Sun God Vivasvan, who sustains life on earth. He then shared it with his son Manu who, in turn, shared it with his son King Iksvaku.'

This chain of teaching was continued through royal kings and saints as per ancient tradition. The 5,000-year-old message of Karm Yoga was then shared with everyone without discrimination, so that they could understand the value of human birth and achieve a higher state of life.

Key Elements: Heritage of Excellence

The ancient yet timeless discipline of Karm Yoga is a 360-degree approach to engaging with karm and its ecosystem to empower the *karta* or the doer, irrespective of the nature, amount, or location of work. Indeed, it offers a clear, sophisticated yet flexible path of approaching one's work-life, driven by an evolved attitude, a deep commitment to goals, and a sustained long-term effort to achieve them.

At its core is the powerful belief that everyone has the potential to be the best version of themselves and to achieve true success—both in their personal and professional lives.

Think about it. If one is underperforming at work or not utilizing their full potential, can they ever feel truly successful? They cannot, can they? This is why work has been viewed as an instrument to achieve contentment, success, and peace since time immemorial.

No wonder, then, that it was considered the first step towards leading a satisfying and meaningful life by many philosophers and leaders, such as Swami Vivekananda, Mahatma Gandhi and Sarojini Naidu, amongst others.

But, surprisingly, many laypeople and most in the business world know little of this powerful philosophy and its profound impact on performance, morale, leadership, success, and quality of life. They remain unaware of its potential as a valuable source of inspiration at home and in the workplace, more so in the post-pandemic, war-stricken global economy.

How can it help the layperson and the leader alike? Well, the primary goals of both these groups are joy, power, wealth, fame, growth, and success. They may nurture the desire to enhance their asset base with the acquisition of real estate, cars, gadgets, etc., to nurture the family unit, and to earn and save for the future. Karm Yoga encourages them to strive for these goals and to discharge their responsibilities towards the self, family, occupation, and community. It is necessary to engage and direct energies, otherwise an idle mind will move towards indulgence or wrong actions, as more often than not that is its nature. This can be avoided by building and nurturing what I call the Work Quotient.

The Work Quotient

The Work Quotient is a set of key physical, emotional, and spiritual traits and qualities considered vital in the implementation of Karm Yoga.

It has the power to nurture the younger generation of employees at the threshold of their careers, enabling them to perform with excellence, while offering a roadmap of growth and development to middle-level managers in the householder stage of life. For the top management or CEOs responsible for leading their organizations, it can serve as a model of transformation and a visionary beacon for a brighter future. Thus, it can help each and every person find meaningful success and joy with the combination of intelligence and emotional and work quotients.

However, it does not include those traits that encourage success at any cost or drive one to engage in 'wrong' work, act without integrity, or be a workaholic. One is not considered a karm yogi with a well-developed Work Quotient if the goal is unethical, even if one performs it in a dedicated manner.

This is because to practise Karm Yoga with a strong Work Quotient, success needs to be attained responsibly, without harming others and without compromising on one's principles and values.

One may wonder, what is defined as success? In modern times, success refers to the acquisition of maximum wealth, fame, influence, assets, and power. Everyone wants to 'get it all' and 'have it all' by any means necessary.

But the principles of Karm Yoga do not consider success driven purely by hostile ambition and devoid of ethics or spirituality as genuine in the true sense of the word. They view it in a nuanced and elevated manner. According to them:

- Doing the right thing without worrying about results—the performance of duty with an elevated attitude—is success.
- Giving and sharing is success.
- Being comfortable physically, mentally, and spiritually with the self is success.
- Being joyful and peaceful in the moment is success.
- Inculcating love, faith, compassion, and gratitude is success.
- Ensuring the joy of loved ones and team members and taking care of them is success.
- Excellence with no compromise on quality is success.

When everyone has achieved success, one will too. Till then, one's duties must be performed. How a person thinks and behaves in the journey of empowerment while nurturing the Work Quotient is success; it is not about just reaching the destination. One can feel successful on a daily basis and accomplish both material and spiritual goals by practising Karm Yoga. Success is not dependent on the recognition or validation of the world, rather it is a sense of accomplishment and achievement that one must feel from within. Elevated action and a higher purpose can also ensure that one's next life is successful.

However, it is commonly, albeit wrongly, assumed that living and working in this manner is not compatible with worldly goals.

There are many other misconceptions regarding Karm Yoga, or even regarding what the Gita says in general, such as:

- It discourages success, ambition, fame, and wealth.
- It classifies all desire as harmful.
- It encourages renunciation of work.
- It is impractical and not relevant to our times.
- It appeals only to the older generation.

Nothing can be further from the truth. As we go ahead, we will observe that Karm Yoga with a strong Work Quotient is perfectly suited to this age of distraction, as it offers a comprehensive solution to many social ills. It is aimed at the householder and the worker for whom desire is important. It forbids them from giving up work and encourages ambition and success. Thus, it is practical, timely, and relevant; although rooted in ancient times, its essence and soul is perfectly suited to modern times.

However, I believe the modern economic philosophy is ego-driven, selfish, and destructive. It has destabilized and distorted the mindset and potential of the individual, the workplace, and the society. It has led to serious problems like lopsided growth, #MeToo incidents, harassment, and race-, gender-, and caste-based discrimination that deeply affect the health and longevity of the careers of those at the receiving end, the colleagues who witness them, their families, and the community. They illustrate the distorted nature of the work–worker–leader relationship, which seems stuck in a time warp, and functions through fear or manipulation rather than respect and collaboration. But it is not a sustainable approach. Thankfully, discrimination, mistreatment, abuse, a selfish mindset, and lack of diversity are no longer acceptable or excusable.

This modern way of working is now also being blamed

for many a lifestyle disease and heart attack, which have become common in the 20–40 age group. A 2021 study conducted by the World Health Organization (WHO) and International Labour Organization (ILO) showed that those who worked for 55 hours a week or more were at a higher risk of dying early compared to their peers. This was also true for those who worked overtime every day, and it was attributed to a mix of poor diet, a sedentary lifestyle, and high occupational stress.[1] This is a common and sorry statistic for many a new-age 'work warrior' and leader across countries and corporations.

This is no longer acceptable or satisfactory to the youth, who are clear about their aspirations and will not hesitate to fulfil them. It's a good time to ask what they want.

Well, surveys have shown that they want more out of life, out of their time, and out of their work. They want to make empowered life choices, discard old practices, reassess career goals, and revisit the meaning of success and work–life balance. Financial stability is important of course, but after a certain point it is not enough of a motivator to remain on the beaten path.

Unsatisfied with both the pre- and the post-pandemic work culture, 95 per cent of the workers surveyed in 2021 by jobs site Monster.com were looking to change jobs and 92 per cent were willing to change industries for the right role. A 2020 Gallup poll revealed that 74 per cent of the millennials (people between the ages of 23 and 38) surveyed

---

[1] 'Long Working Hours Can Increase Deaths from Heart Disease and Stroke, say ILO and WHO', *International Labour Organization*, 17 May 2021, https://tinyurl.com/zhjbh62m. Accessed on 10 June 2024.

did not want to return to office full-time, the highest in any age group.[2]

The writing on the wall is clear! Change is necessary, and it needs to go beyond a temporary stop-gap arrangement or a new policy document that only remains on paper. What also cannot remain is the thought process of modern society that continues to use only the bottom line as a yardstick of success while ignoring its human component.

Why Is this Happening Now?

The pandemic, financial instability, the Ukraine–Russia and Israel–Hamas wars, and the turmoil in Sudan and other parts of the world have changed the world beyond recognition. The way work is performed, the kind of work required, how and where it is performed, the models and technologies with which it is performed, and the ecosystems in which these exist have all changed, and so must the mindset.

The post-pandemic era offers a good opportunity to do so, as it is easier to affect change after tumultuous events. But if people do not reimagine and reinterpret their relationship with work, with themselves, and with each other, then turmoil or not, no new model, philosophy, or technology will stand a chance. If they cannot initiate change within themselves, how will they do so in others and in the world?

---

[2]Cooban, Anna, '95% of Workers Are Thinking About Quitting Their Jobs, According to a New Survey—and Burnout Is the Number One Reason', *Business Insider India*, 7 July 2021, https://tinyurl.com/2pzm94ec. Accessed on 10 June 2024; Robison, Jennifer, 'Will Millennials Finally Get the Workplace They Want?', *Gallup*, 13 November 2020, https://tinyurl.com/vf8pedjh. Accessed on 22 May 2024.

At a Crossroads: Reimagining the Way Forward

It is at this juncture that Karm Yoga comes in. It gently inspires change-makers to initiate the process of change within themselves so that they can become the instrument and embodiment of true success. It inspires a profound elevation of thought, action, and consciousness to ensure one's work-life sparks meaningful success, joy, and contentment. It does so by placing the wellness of all the stakeholders at the heart of action—that is, by placing purpose over profit, since a society is only as good as the vision and the mindset of its people.

Daniel Jebasingh, the managing director of Covenant Consultants, a leading manpower consulting firm, and ex-chief human resource officer (CHRO) of Consim Info, shared his view on the importance of a purpose-driven life, based on his rich experience of recruiting for C-level (top management) positions:

> I have seen so many CEOs at the peak of their careers who are unsatisfied with their lives. Although they have achieved everything, after heading the best organizations, earning big pay cheques with multiple houses, fame, success, etc., they still feel empty within. Many are leaving their high-powered jobs after 20–30 years in search of this elusive satisfaction. I believe this stems from an absence of a larger purpose, rather the lack of a calling, without which material success will always seem insufficient.[3]

---

[3] Conveyed personally to the author.

This brings us to the futility of over-emphasizing profit and material achievement at the cost of everything else, which ultimately leaves one dissatisfied and unhappy, unable to function like a leader and incapable of feeling truly successful.

But who is a real leader anyway? According to Vivek Jalan, a headhunter and founding managing partner at Talent Sharks, a boutique executive search firm: 'Apart from meeting all the usual attributes as expected, a leader must possess strengths in soft skills—comfort with ambiguity, ability to build a diverse team, conflict resolution, ability to communicate with the business owners and other key stakeholders in a democratic way.'[4]

The composite of all these strengths makes one a leader, not just a fancy designation or a corner office.

The Karm Yoga Lessons and their Work Quotient inspire everyone to live life to the fullest like a leader, and to achieve real success by serving as catalysts for re-engineering the mindset. Yes, they encourage ambition, wealth, and growth, but through ethical means. This requires a complete transformation of thought and action and cannot be inculcated overnight; it is not a quick fix. And its implementation is not one-size-fits-all, as every person is different.

For a successful work-life, one can prepare the self to walk down the path of Karm Yoga by practising the first two points, and then imbibing its 7 Lessons:

1. Mindset management: awareness of the self and one's potential, occupational duties, and duty towards health

---

[4]Conveyed personally to the author.

2. Role within society: compulsory social duties
3. The 7 Lessons and their implementation

Understanding the Nature of Work

na hi kaschit kshanam api jatu tishtahtyakarmkrit
karyate hyavasha karm sarvah prakriti jair gunaih

(Bhagavad Gita 3:5)

Let's begin by understanding what work is, what initiates it or what its seed is, what types of actions it consists of, and what the results of the wrong way of working are. Karm Yoga states that the seed of all work is desire. As the quoted section from the Gita states, every being functions due to the modes of nature, filled with desire. No one can refrain from action for even a moment.

Without desire, no task is performed and no one is motivated to act. It is desire that inspires one to acquire, leave, make or change something, set one's goals, and work on them till they are achieved. One may use different actions to do so and they are classified into four categories: *utpaadya*, the action that leads to creation; *sanskaarya*, the action that leads to improvement; *vikaarya*, the action that changes the look and form, creating something new; and *aapya*, the action of seeking assistance to get work done.

When these actions are initiated by a selfish desire, one may develop false ego and pride. After one achieves the goal, one may think along these lines: 'I alone did it', 'I crushed my competitors', 'I won by hook or crook, so what', and 'I am better than others'. Thought processes like these demonstrate that one has developed attachment to duty and is being driven by ego, which will have a binding effect.

Thus, the result of the act driven by desire is attachment.

dhyayato vishayan pumsah sangas teshupajayate
sangaat sanjayate kamah kamat krodho bhijayate

(Bhagavad Gita 2:62)

That is, when one desires something, one develops an attachment to it that evokes lust, followed by anger.

This does not mean that one should not care for the work at hand, but that one should engage with it in the right way. Is there only one right way? No, there are many different kartas or doers, and they may engage in different ways across geographies, economies, and businesses.

Recognizing this diversity, ancient Indian philosophy and yogic tradition suggested a choice of different paths depending on one's personality, nature, culture, and lifestyle. The thought process behind this was 'your route is right for you, my route is right for me'. The ultimate goal remained the same; no matter what country one belonged to or the beliefs one practised, it could be achieved with dedication and faith.

There are three key routes to success and empowerment suggested in the Gita: Gyan Yoga, the art of knowledge; Karm Yoga, the art of work; and Bhakti Yoga, the art of devotion.

For the one who is action-oriented, the path of Karm Yoga is suggested, which ensures financial and spiritual success.

7 Lessons of Karm Yoga: The Future of Work

Karm Yoga can be practised with the support of its eternal lessons, which are:

1. Discharge all the duties (*swadharma* or the duty mindset)
2. Duties must be discharged intelligently (Buddhi Yoga mindset)
3. Duties must be discharged in the framework of yogic action and treated akin to worship (faith mindset)
4. Wrongful or *adharmic* actions must be avoided or reduced, and good or *dharmic* activities must be increased (dharmic vs adharmic mindset)
5. Duties that lead to community welfare must be increased (*loka sangraha* mindset)
6. Work must not be done only for the fruits of the action (*abhokta* or the non-enjoyer mindset)
7. The ego must be surrendered; the individual must not believe they are the doer (*akarta* or the non-doer mindset)

If one finds it challenging to implement all the teachings at once, they can discharge them in part or as best as possible. The teachings are not mutually exclusive but flow into one another as one continues with their duty. Practising them and embarking on this journey in the spirit of yoga is more important than the speed of implementation.

A word of caution here—the challenges of work-life will not disappear by adopting the 7 Lessons. An aspiring karm yogi's life will have its fair share of problems. But since their mind will be strengthened with Karm Yoga, they will view them as opportunities and succeed in managing them. Thus, Karm Yoga will not reduce or change the material challenges of the world, but enhance one's capacity and ability to navigate them.

> ### KEY TAKEAWAYS
> - All activities of life are called karm or work.
> - The seed of work is desire.
> - The result of work is attachment, if driven by false ego.
> - The elevated approach to life and work is called Karm Yoga.
> - Karm Yoga can address the problems inherent in modern society.

MINDSET MANAGEMENT: BECOMING A KARM YOGI

1
Understanding the Self
Mindset Management through the Three Gunas

asato maa sad gamaya, tamso maa jyotir gamaya, mrityor maa amritam gamaya. Om shanti, shanti, shantihi.

[Lead me from untruth to truth, from darkness to light, and from death to eternity. Om peace, peace, peace.]

(Brihadaranyaka Upanishad 1.3.28)

In the Introduction, we discussed the explanation offered by the principles of Karm Yoga about the seed of work and its result when it is desire-driven. Next, we focus on mindset management, which includes understanding the self and managing one's health.

This chapter focusses on the first part: understanding and managing the self.

Understanding the Self: Role of Gunas

As mentioned earlier, work must be performed in the spirit of yoga even though its seed is desire. Yes, the world moves due to desire, but what inspires it?

Work is driven by the three gunas: sattva-guna, rajo-guna

and tamo-guna. These three attributes are present in every being in different proportions and inspire or influence all action and thought. They make their presence felt through different actions; this is why they are called the 'drivers' of work.

sattvam rajas tama iti gunah prakriti sambhavah
nibadhnanti mahabaho dehe dehinam avyayam

(Bhagavad Gita 14:5)

That is, nature has three gunas or modes and all beings are conditioned by them. Their characteristics are:

1. **Prakash (light) or sattva-guna:** Knowledge, inner peace, stability, mercy, empathy and amity
2. **Kriya (action) or rajo-guna:** Movement, effort, competition, attempt and ambition
3. **Stithi (stillness) or tamo-guna:** Incompetence, oversleeping, lack of knowledge, idleness and excessive rest

Gunas in Action: As the Drivers of Work

This is how gunas drive action and thought:

Sattva-guna

When a person works hard, makes sacrifices to finish a project before the deadline, and supports their team or family, they are being sattvik in nature. Sattva-guna is dominant in them. It keeps their mind alert, thoughtful, and free from disturbances.

tatra satvam nirmalatvat prakashakam anamayam
sukha sangena badhnati gyana sangena cha anagha

(Bhagavad Gita 14:6)

That is, this mode is steeped in light and free from sin; one in this mode is happy and filled with knowledge.

Both in their personal and professional life, the sattva-guni person knows how to manage themselves. They are wary of the excess pleasure that comes from indulgence. They are calm, mindful and able to control their sense organs in the face of temptation. They control their tongue, both while consuming food and communicating. They know what to say, how much to say, and when to stay silent. The more they learn, the more they realize how little they know.

They exercise control over what they consume, neither over- nor under-eating. They avoid anything that is bad for their health or does not suit them. This includes indulgence in social media, which they regulate effectively.

Rajo-guna

When one initiates multiple projects and struggles with different activities and goals, one is being rajsik in nature. Rajo-guna is dominant in a preoccupied mind filled with desires and selfish ambition.

rajo ragatmakam vidhi trishna sanga samudbhavam
tan nibhadnati kaunteya karm sangena dehinam

(Bhagavad Gita 14:7)

That is, one in this mode has unending desires and is tied to their actions.

The rajo-guni is not as adept at self-management as the sattvik person. They are focussed on personal pleasure and self-indulgence. Their desire to enjoy is like nectar in the beginning and poison towards the end—that is, they end up with attachment and suffering.

For instance, at a buffet a rajo-guni person with poor digestion may be overcome with desire. Their eyes take in the sight of the food, the mind communicates its hunger, and their nose enjoys the delicious aroma. These sense organs overpower the brain and drive them to indulge, although they know it is wrong to do so.

Later, they suffer from indigestion, stomach pain, and discomfort. The end result of this pattern of indulgence in food or any other temptation is disease and sorrow, both in the short and long run.

Tamo-guna

When one prefers sleeping on the job or at home, or just coasts through the day with minimum effort, one is being tamsik in nature. Tamo-guna is dominant in such a person. Their mind avoids thinking or planning and is not receptive to knowledge.

tamas tv agyana jam viddhi mohanam sarva dehinaam
pramaad aalasya nidrabhis tan nibhadnati bharata

(Bhagavad Gita 14:8)

That is, one in this mode suffers from laziness, over-sleeping and ignorance.

A tamo-guni is hopeless at self-management. They like to indulge their senses and obey their desires, rather than doing what should be done. They may have a few goals, but are unable to achieve any of them. This is because they may be unmotivated, or their mind may not be sharp enough to do so. The worst part is that they do not make an effort to push themselves.

Clearly the sattva-guni is better at self- and work-management compared to the rajo-guni, who is better at it than a tamo-guni person.

By understanding and monitoring the self, one can understand which guna is driving one's actions. If one aspires to be successful and is in the lowest stage of tamo-guna, one must first move up to the rajo-guna stage. Then, one can seek to progress to the higher stage of sattva-guna. The goal being to reduce excess tamo-guna, balance rajo-guna, and increase sattva-guna.

Right Mix of Gunas: The Stages of Action

There are different combinations of gunas, but only the highest stage can lead to success (Stage 1 being the lowest and Stage 4 being the highest stage of action):

1. **Stage 1 (tamo-guna > rajo-guna > sattva-guna):** If one has a dominance of tamo-guna, a small amount of rajo-guna, and scarce sattva-guna, one is in Stage 1. Such a person may be lethargic and given to sporadic bursts of activity. They may not be focussed or driven to achieve their goals due to the excess of tamo-guni tendencies. If they seek to advance, they must begin by practising Karm Yoga with a *sakaam* attitude, or working for the results. They must increase their

rajo-guni desires and engage with worldly duties, as it is better than non-action. Once they become sufficiently active, they can move to Stage 2.

2. **Stage 2 (rajo-guna > tamo-guna > sattva-guna):** In this stage, since the person has become active, there is a dominance of rajo-guna, some amount of tamo-guna, and a sprinkling of sattva-guna. To progress, they should attempt *nishkaam* Karm Yoga, that is, perform the duty without a focus on results. They may then begin to acquire wealth and fame due to excessive rajsik tendencies. But they must not only take from society, they also need to evolve and give back to it. They must elevate their thought process and balance material and spiritual success. When this happens, they will be ready to move on to the next stage of growth.

3. **Stage 3 (rajo-guna > sattva-guna > tamo-guna):** In this stage, the person is an active contributor. There is a dominance of rajo-guna, some amount of sattva-guna, and a scarce amount of tamo-guna. They should continue engaging with their duties but practise meditation to keep themselves calm. They must also reduce their overtly extroverted nature, which can divert their mind from the goals, and prepare for Stage 4.

4. **Stage 4 (sattva-guna > rajo-guna > tamo-guna):** When a person reaches this stage, they already exert a fair amount of control on their mind. They are filled with knowledge and goodness, and a small amount of rajo-guna and tamo-guna. One must now attempt to reduce the dominance of all three gunas and utilize the gunas' power without coming under their control. A person must continue to enhance their wisdom, deeply contemplate

their role and the nature of the world, and seek a higher purpose. This is freedom for an evolved mind and highlights the person's growth on the pathway of Karm Yoga.

Thus, Stage 4 offers the perfect combination of the three gunas, and nurtures the right mindset towards action and success.

Some fine examples of Stage 4 karm yogis were Mahatma Gandhi, Nelson Mandela, Martin Luther King, Jr., and Helen Keller. They were and are admired, not only in their respective countries but all over the world, because their beliefs and actions transcended boundaries. True, they were born with unique traits, but they were able to nurture many others to fulfil their potential; this enabled them to achieve larger-than-life goals.

Gandhi's Approach to His Karm or Duty

Mahatma Gandhi was driven by the principles of humanity, equity, truth, and social justice. He was dedicated to the Indian independence struggle and as a result was imprisoned several times and suffered greatly at the hands of the British rulers. But he never gave up on his principles or his vision of freedom for the country. Was it because he was expecting a big bonus or a palatial house as a reward? No, he was merely performing his duty.

He functioned like a karm yogi leader by placing the interests of the people before his own in the spirit of loka sangraha (Lesson 5), and practised Buddhi Yoga by performing his duty—that is, by using non-violence

(Lessons 1 and 2); he did not work solely for the fruits of his actions (Lesson 6). Further, he did not consider himself the doer, which demonstrated a reduced ego (Lesson 7). This enabled him to bring together leaders and numerous followers from different walks of life, transforming his movement into a pan-India struggle.

Then, even during the most difficult times, when it appeared impossible, he persevered and his yogic attitude transformed him from a common man into the Father of the Nation.

His sattvik nature and the principles of Karm Yoga that he followed enabled him to fulfil a higher purpose, and he succeeded in liberating India from the clutches of colonialism in 1947.

Gandhi's life is a clear example of how one can succeed with an elevated mindset towards duty and by managing the gunas.

Why the Lower Gunas Must Be Managed

The great Indian philosopher and saint Swami Vivekananda also stressed on the importance of managing the gunas. He often encouraged his followers to play football instead of reading the Gita. What did this signify? Well, he did not suggest that one should not read the sacred book. What he wanted to convey was that one should reduce tamo-guna; he did not want people to use the Gita as a cover for their lethargy. Instead of this stage of inaction, he wanted people to shift to the higher stage of action with football.

Indeed, tamo-guna is the source of many modern problems, so one may be tempted to conclude that it should be wiped out completely. But it plays an important role as it drives sleep and is vital for the normal functioning of the body. Without sleep and rest, the mind and body will not be rejuvenated and can fall prey to disease. No medicine can compensate for the absence of sleep, thus it needs to be maintained in proportion with other gunas.

This is easier said than done, though, as sleep problems have become common in contemporary society. Anecdotal evidence suggests that sleep problems of some form or another are rising and increasing stress levels, health concerns, and economic miseries. This is concerning, as it can be a precursor to complications in the future.

To avoid such a scenario, tamo-guna needs to be maintained, albeit in a small amount, with a dominance of sattva-guna (Stage 4 of action). But it is not easy to be sattvik in modern society, focussed as it is on rajo-guni activities.

Similarly, rajo-guna should be maintained in proportion or it can lead to an increase of intense actions and unending desires fuelled by anger, unchecked ambition, and dissatisfaction. This is why it is common to witness many people who are dominated by rajo-guna and excess desire always struggling to accomplish some goal or another, filled with lust, greed, fear, insecurity, anxiety, and stress.

One may wonder why that is a problem, as it is considered normal to be in a state of constant struggle and stress in the digital age. But these emotions, lower gunas, and unchecked desires can pose impediments to a life of purpose, sacrifice, discipline, and success.

How Desire Behaves in the Gunas

> *dhumenavriyate vahnir yathadarsho malena cha*
> *yatholbenavrito garbhastatha tenedam avritam*

(Bhagavad Gita 3:38)

The above quote reflects that as smoke covers the fire, a mirror is covered by dust, and the embryo is covered by the womb; in the same way, a person is covered by different layers of desire. Let's see how rajo-guna inspires desire and how the above-mentioned emotions arise in different groups.

In a Sattva-guni Person

In a sattvik person, desire is like a fire with smoke around it. When something burns, both the fire and the smoke around it are visible. Tempted by desire, the sattvik one remembers their duty, work, and knowledge. The fire of knowledge is visible to them, however the desire in the form of smoke may try its best to cover it. But if they are strong, they can avoid giving in to the desire and defeat it using pure knowledge.

It is not that they never give in to desire or anger, or that they never make a mistake. Everyone faces the same set of desires, more or less, but the sattvik one is aware of their presence and effect. Even when they are giving in to their desires, they recognize when they have exceeded their self-imposed limit or committed a sin. They are then able to stop the indulgence and get back on track.

Thus, they are able to work and live with self-control, and not let their desires get the better of them. Further, they do not allow anger to disturb them or make their decisions for them; it is a tool that they use to further their goals.

The sattva-guni person who aspires to be successful has the right attitude towards work. They are pleased to engage with it; their joy is different and elevated. It does not come easy but they do not complain. Rather, they learn to enjoy the effort their work requires. When distracted by sense pleasure, they restrain themselves and refresh their focus. The hard work is like poison to them in the beginning. Initially, they do miss the fun and the overindulgence in food and drink. But with time, they learn to navigate their desires and focus on the duty.

Collaborative in nature, they work along with their team (or family) with a clear goal in mind. They are active and driven, and do not give up when faced with problems. They think innovatively, persevere in the face of challenges, and maintain a positive attitude. They troubleshoot and redesign plans if the situation changes, as they have a Plan B in hand. They understand their customers and share insights to design clear campaigns or solutions.

A team comprising such sattvik workers achieves the goal on schedule, and their excellent work is recognized and commended by all.

This gives a sattvic person real pleasure or higher joy, and it tastes like nectar in the end. Afterwards, they may enjoy some much-needed downtime and unwind with friends and family, for they know when leisure needs to be prioritized; they are not boring or dull but strategic in approach.

Sattvik joy ties one to hard work, just like rajsik joy ties one to desire. Ethical work, social work, and one's duty are considered higher actions that are driven by *gyan* or knowledge. An example of a sattvik leader in modern times was former president A.P.J. Abdul Kalam, who inspired the nation through his life of excellence and service.

In a Rajo-guni Person

Desire appears like a mirror covered with dust for a rajo-guni person. When the mirror is dirty, they cannot see their reflection. But when they wipe some of the dust with their finger, the small portion that is clean shows their reflection. This is symbolic of the duties that they remember, whereas the covered larger portion represents the part of them that is controlled by desire.

A big part of the rajo-guni person's mind is filled with desire, and more often than not they give in to it, thinking that they are doing the right thing. They live a life controlled by external influences and are unable to reach their full potential. They do not perform their prescribed duties, and spend more time satisfying their desires.

Since they are action-oriented, they contribute to society through their initiatives. They drive growth and prosperity with their diverse operations, although their mind is restless while engaged in them. Such a person is quick to lose their temper and suffers the consequences that arise from the lack of self-control and frequent indulgence in desire.

The rajo-guni person who aspires to be successful wants to achieve many goals in life, which is an admirable work ethic. But this makes their mind unsteady, as they are not able to prioritize and end up struggling with many different desires at the same time.

Consequently, they are busy on a never-ending quest to acquire things, experiences, and people, but are never satisfied and are always 'on the hunt'; they remain unsteady and are unable to experience real joy.

Yes, they work hard but it is for the sole aim of wealth and selfish ambition. They desire to win either by hook or by crook, do not believe in collaboration, and dislike their competitors. What is worse, they do not care about the welfare of the community, and if they participate in social responsibility initiatives, they are driven by the desire for fame or power. An example of a rajo-guni leader is the modern politician or businessman, who works with the motive of profit and does not care about the long-term impact of their actions on the community.

For instance, energy company Enron's founder, CEO, and chairman Kenneth Lay was a rajo-guni leader. He presided over its rapid growth and under his leadership it was declared 'America's Most Innovative Company' by *Fortune* magazine six times in a row between 1996 and 2001. It also won the 'Energy Company of the Year' award in 2001 from the *Financial Times*. But by 2006, his house of cards came crashing down. He indulged in a number of wrongful actions that led to the downfall of the company, and was later convicted of securities and wire fraud by the US courts.

In a Tamo-guni Person

Desire covers a tamo-guni person completely like the body covers an organ. A tamo-guni individual is desire personified. Their mind is unsteady and they spend all their time trying to fulfil their every wish. They are not able to differentiate right from wrong. They believe that they are a victim of life and function without self-control. They avoid hard work and make excuses for their failures. Since they are not able to achieve their goals, sorrow is a big part of their life.

They are easily angered, and this is another reason why they are not able to progress. It stops them from collaborating with others; their ego and foolishness also get the better of them. Thus, desire and anger are their enemies, but they believe these are their allies, that they are good for them. They are not able to understand their true nature and keep chasing desires.

Comfort is important to them and they ensure that they never have to struggle or invest effort, even if it causes problems later. They enjoy stimulants, addictive products, and other harmful substances that offer temporary pleasure. In this way, they fall further into the clutches of tamo-guna, degrading their mental and physical health.

The tamo-guni person who aspires to be successful is excessively attached to their tasks, but does not work smart. Note that it is their false ego that is controlled by desire and not the *atma* or soul, as that remains pure.

When assigned an important duty, they feel or show no enthusiasm. They prefer being idle while pretending to work and actually enjoy wasting time. Their mind is focussed on how they can entertain themselves or how they can indulge their senses. They may often pretend to be unwell, and miss work and meetings as a result. Sadly, they may be aware of the importance of excellence but are unable to deliver it. If and when they are forced to act, they commit mistakes, as they are distracted. And they continue to drift aimlessly across projects, jobs, and relationships.

Often, they hand over their duties to the team or family without being aware of their capability to perform them. The latter suffer due to the former's wrong decisions, driven by a lack of knowledge. Such a tamo-guni person avoids taking responsibility if something goes wrong and indulges in blame games. Their team members are demotivated, not inspired to work, and unable to achieve their goals.

An example of a tamo-guni leader is Kim Jong Un, the supreme leader of North Korea, who has plunged his nation into hunger and chaos, and adversely affected its economic, social, and cultural development.

Another tamo-guni leader was Adolf Hitler, a dictator who ruled Germany from 1933 to 1947. Instead of bringing his people together, he tried to divide them on the basis of race and ethnicity. His huge ego, uncontrollable desire to dominate the world, and lust for violence demonstrated his intense rajo-guni and tamo-guni tendencies. These tendencies nurtured uncontrolled ambition that blinded him to the greater good and led him to destroy the cultural fabric of his nation. Driven by an insatiable thirst for power, he led his country into World War II, one of the most devastating conflicts of all time. The rest, as they say, is history. Even today, his life serves as a cautionary tale as to how one man with a deplorable mindset can destroy millions of lives.

These real-life examples of sattva-guni, tamo-guni and rajo-guni leaders demonstrate the far-reaching impact of the gunas and how they impact not only the individual, but also their family, country, and the world.

To Sum Up Briefly

In the different gunas, desire and anger express themselves in different ways and adversely affect those under their grip.

A sattva-guni worker is mildly troubled by their desires, a rajo-guni is very troubled by them, and a tamo-guni person is a bundle of desires, living an uncontrolled and uncomfortable life.

*karmanah sukritasyahuh sattvikam nirmalam phalam
rajasastu phalam dukham agyanam tamasa phalam*

(Bhagavad Gita 14:16)

That is, the result of higher action is purity, of rajsik action is misery, and of tamsik action is folly.

Thus, desire troubles every person but it is up to the individual to manage it.

Rising Rajo-guna: Managing the Many-Headed Monster of Desire

All desire is driven by rajo-guna and fuelled by *kalpana* or imagination. Since it can take many forms, it is difficult to identify which are ethical and which are not, and how they will affect a person.

For instance, when one falls in love, one assumes that the other can offer happiness or security in the form of friendship or companionship. Or if one is drawn to another's physical attributes, they may want to possess the other for their own pleasure. These actions are driven by desire and the need to please the self; tendencies that are strong when the mind becomes rajsik and that can push one towards needing many different objects and people.

If the person is not careful, these desires can trap them in a maze of greed, sorrow, and disillusionment. They may then blame other people, neighbours, loved ones, friends, companies, or products, but they should know that they are the cause of their sorrow and only they can be the solution.

Karm Yoga explains that one needs to blame the incessant and powerful desires in the mind, as these are the starting point of most troubles.

yatato hyapi kaunteya purushasya vipaschitaha
indriyani pramathini haranti prasabham manah

(Bhagavad Gita 2:60)

That is, the senses are so overcome by desire that they can forcibly sway even an intelligent person's mind.

Not all desires are harmful, but giving in to all of them is. However, a modern householder or worker is not used to hearing no or leaving their desire unmet. It starts small: first, they desire to be recognized as the best in their team, then in their company, and then to be promoted to the leadership ranks. After that, they desire to consolidate their power and wealth.

Next, they may dream of becoming a millionaire, and following that, a billionaire. As a billionaire, they may desire to control the world, the metaverse, other planets, and so on.

Elon Musk, a billionaire entrepreneur heading distinguished corporations like Tesla, Space X, etc., is regarded as one of the richest and most powerful men in the world. His next goal? To colonize Mars and make humanity multi-planetary. His intentions may or may not work out, but they are a good example of how desires do not end even after one achieves all that is possible on Earth.

The point being that whether one is a leader or worker, rich or poor, powerful or weak, all are and will be unsatisfied with their current standing in life. Thus, even after amassing all the wealth and power in this planet (and on other planets), one's desires will never end and they will keep struggling to meet them. It is a vicious cycle, one that most are happy to be a part of. They are unaware that even after fulfilling their desire they will be unable to find true joy and meaning in their existence, as there will be a barrage of new desires waiting to take over.

This is not to discourage ambition but to illustrate the nature of desires, which are distorted by greed, selfishness, and ego. But understanding them is not enough to tame them, especially in this age of disruption and distraction, where instant pleasure, aggression, and over-accumulation of wealth are considered normal and even encouraged.

Indeed, financial success is important, but when one's obsession with it goes out of hand, it brings sorrow and anger in its wake. It increases the lower gunas and decreases the probability of true success and happiness.

kama krodha vimuktanam yatinam yata chetasam
abhito brahma nirvanam vartate viditatmanaam

(Bhagavad Gita 5:26)

That is, only the one who is free from anger and desire, and is disciplined and self-realized, will be able to achieve liberation and success.

However, desire also drives one to work. Thus, the inherent problem is that if one gives it up, no one will strive to accomplish anything and there will be no discoveries or inventions. No new product or service will be created and society will not be able to advance.

So, ambition and rajo-guna are crucial attributes but they must be balanced with the desire to achieve success selflessly and ethically.

With the Karm Yoga Lessons and the Work Quotient qualities nurtured by it (explained in Chapters 4–10), it is possible to do so and accomplish the four goals of life.

Goals of Life vs Desire

Indian philosophy lays stress on achieving all the four goals of life, or *purushaarth*s, which are: *arth, kaam, dharma* and *moksha*. Arth is the pursuit of wealth, kaam is desire, dharma is one's elevated nature and moksha is self-actualization.

Since ancient times, moksha was considered the highest goal of life, as it denoted freedom from the cycle of birth and rebirth. But today, few pursue moksha because they are unaware of its importance. Dharma is also low on the to-do list, as it is difficult to discharge all of one's duties and involves placing the interests of the community or others before one's own. It does ensure big rewards, but they take time to fructify and sometimes bear fruit in the next birth or after that.

Most people aspiring for success are restless; they want immediate results. They do not want to wait for the benefits to start accruing. What will they do with the benefits in the next life? They are unable to postpone their pleasure and want to enjoy in the moment. But that is not mindfulness, rather it is a mindless gratification of the senses.

Thus, they focus on the first two goals of arth and kaam that are driven by desire. This helps them achieve financial stability and meet the needs of the family. This is important, as it is one's duty to take care of loved ones. While doing so, the individual must accept ethical profits and fame when they are well-deserved, but avoid hankering after them because it will allow desire to morph into different emotions.

If one's desire is driven by indulgence and acquisition, when it is disturbed or prevented it transforms into anger. If fulfilled, one's desire turns into greed. Unchecked anger, desire, and greed have grave consequences and are called the three gates to hell in the Gita:

trividham narakasyedam dwaram naashanam aatmanah
kaamah krodhas tatha lobhas tasmad etat trayam tyajet

(Bhagavad Gita 16:21)

When one desires something and is unable to achieve it, and when faced with an opponent more powerful, the desire turns into fear. The base is still desire, but it is an unfulfilled one, thwarted due to the power and larger desire of one's opponent. Thus, it is kaam or desire that becomes fear with a bigger opponent or problem, becomes greed with indulgence, and turns into anger when denied.

How can anger be managed? If an individual struggles regularly to manage their anger, they must introspect ('Why do I react like this?') and analyse the cause of their volatility ('Is it always the other person[s] at fault or is it my own set of unending desires that make me uncontrollable? Is it my unsteady nature that makes me a victim of my own anger?'), as anger first harms the person who is enraged, before harming the one it is directed towards. This behaviour is a sign that rajo-guna has increased and fused with tamo-guna, caging one in rage and fear. Such an individual should fear themselves and their impulsiveness, which makes them reckless and unpredictable.

Such behaviour will certainly make them unreliable and unpopular with their family or team members, who will not know what may trigger them. The family and team will hesitate to share their frank opinion and the individual will be manipulated by those who know what buttons to press. Further, their image will suffer if they lose self-control in front of the team, society, shareholders, or external vendors. And it will lead to clashes with other leaders or contemporaries when they perform better than the individual; that is, when their desire is fulfilled and not the individual's.

If their anger is always close to boiling point, even a small spark will create a big problem, and they will hurt those they love the most. The loved ones will then distance themselves and slowly drift away from their mercurial temperament.

Thus, anger has the power to damage relationships with those at the receiving end of such an individual's wrath, which will probably be everyone, sooner rather than later. They may try to justify it with righteousness or with logic but the damage will be done by then. It will become their second nature and the frequency of their outbursts will continue to increase.

How I Manage My Gunas: A Personal Example

Understanding rajo-guna helped me enhance my attitude towards work-life and become more focussed and productive.

For instance, on the days I approach my duty with annoyance (if the workload is immense), or anger (if there is a delay in receiving my assignment), or stress (if the deadlines are short), I understand that my rajsik nature is rising and needs to be managed. After all, we spend a large part of our lives engaged in work; isn't it better to do so with joy and positivity, and not stress and anger?

So I take a break—I either go for a walk or read a book. I offer gratitude (which boosts sattva-guna) and remind myself that the duty needs to be performed without excuses, and then begin with an enhanced attitude.

There are also times when I am unhappy or doubtful about the quality of my work, which is upsetting. In my mind, I start to rewrite and edit whatever I am working on at the time, even after submitting it (do not recommend this).

I find it helpful to pause and reflect, to try to understand what is really going on. I realize that once again it is rajo-guna that is creating the set of desires that are troubling me, not the world or the story, novel, or poem I'm working on. I try to accept the situation with a positive, calm attitude, rather than thinking about it on loop.

When I feel demotivated or lack inspiration, I accept that it is the tamo-guna that is rising. It may be due to a genuine reason like fatigue, and sometimes it may be due to plain old lethargy. Taking small breaks or spending time in nature or with a loved one helps. So does choosing not to work on weekends, or indulging in reading or sattvik activities.

What also helps greatly is reducing mindless scrolling on social media, which can increase tamo-guna, and avoiding inflammatory content or arguing with strangers (or known people for that matter), which can boost rajo-guna.

Basically, if we try to engage in sattvik activites and reduce the rajsik and tamsik ones, we will be able to balance the gunas and be more productive. Anyone can work in an elevated manner by managing themselves, so keep at it and the results will speak for themselves.

Defeating Selfish Desire: Saam, Daam, Dand, and Bhed

After understanding the nature of the gunas and how desire behaves in them, a person aspiring for success can use the four tools suggested by ancient Indian philosophy to manage them:

1. **Saam:** This tool involves persuading one to understand the ill-effects of acting on every desire and can be implemented by the control of the sense organs, mind, and brain. For example, the desire to go out during the lockdown was dangerous. So when a friend's young son insisted on going to the park, she had to patiently convince him to play at home. It was not easy, but gentle persuasion did succeed in changing his mind.
2. **Daam:** This involves using financial motivation or an incentive to lure one away from desire. For example, a child may be offered a gift to inspire them to improve their performance at school, or an employee may be selected for the best salesperson award or something along similar

lines upon the achievement of their annual targets. The desire for recognition along with higher pay can motivate the team to work harder.

3. **Dand:** Another possible route is punishment when one cannot reason with an individual or with the self. Should one punish the self? For example, it is common to see a person who ends up overeating go on a punishing diet. But that is not the right approach. The act needs to be punished and avoided, not the person.

4. **Bhed:** This strategy involves exploiting weakness by understanding the self. When an individual is able to separate their desires from themselves, they are able to view the former as a neutral bystander. They can witness their desire rising, becoming strong, and taking over, just like they witness the world around them. They can then prevent it from gaining power. When ignored or denied, the desire will weaken; the mind can reason with the self and banish it.

There are many ways to defeat selfish desire, like the process of abandonment, inaction, separation from the self, detachment, etc.

Crucially, one must nurture the unselfish kaam or good desire with faith or *sradhha* and intelligence. Sraddha is the ability to grasp the truth; it is not blind faith, rather it is an unshakeable belief in oneself and/or in a higher power. It can be a powerful tool to motivate the self and others.

In this way, a person aspiring for success can use the knowledge of the gunas and the nature of desire for self-management and personal growth, at the physical, emotional, and spiritual levels.

KEY TAKEAWAYS

- Gunas drive action: They are present in everyone in different proportions.
- Sattva-guna is superior to rajo-guna, which is better than tamo-guna.
- Desire and anger work differently in the gunas.
- Gunas can be managed with self-control, knowledge, and practice.
- One must manage desire to ensure personal growth.

2

Physical and Mental Wellness

Mindset Management with a Focus on Health

koshto na korle, keshto pava jaye na.

[Without hard work, you cannot attain Krishna.]

—Bengali saying

In the previous chapter, we discussed how by using the tenets of Karm Yoga and with the knowledge of the gunas, one can manage desire. The second aspect of self-management is physical and mental wellness.

Karm Yoga promotes hard work but never at the cost of one's health. Sound physical, spiritual, and mental health is a prerequisite to embarking on this journey, while overworking to the point of harm is the path to failure.

Sadly, some modern philosophers, gurus, and world leaders have glorified overwork and exploited workers for their vested interests. Extremely long hours, inadequate and short breaks, working on weekends and holidays, and no downtime are different forms of overwork that are considered normal today. These affect the mental and physical health of the workers who have no choice but to accept them. This in turn jeopardizes the longevity of their careers, complicates operations, leads to misallocation of resources, and comes at a huge cost to them and society.

Distortion in Relationships: No Work without the Worker

Let's examine this in two ways:

1. the relationship of businesses with those they employ; and
2. the relationship of the leader/worker with their own work and themselves.

Traditional Relationship of Businesses and Workers: Profit over People

As seen commonly, the workplace is characterized by a huge power imbalance, with the bulk of it concentrated in the hands of management. This has led to exploitation, inequity, and undue focus on profit over and above the welfare of the people it employs.

Employees are paid a bare minimum wage in the name of prudent financial management and cost-cutting, while tens of millions are doled out to senior executives in the same breath. The result is that most of the world's resources are concentrated in the hands of this small group of powerful people forming the top 1 per cent, while the remaining 99 per cent struggle to survive. In difficult times, the former's businesses are bailed out, as they are considered too big to fail; but who bails out the worker when they cannot make ends meet? No one.

Unsurprisingly, these workers are fed up with the status quo and are leading protests to bring about radical change. During 2021–23, many chose to leave their jobs across the US and other parts of the world, a phenomenon that was dubbed as the Great Resignation.

In August 2021 alone, around 4.5 million people in the US resigned according to the Job Openings and Labor Turnover Survey, which included workers and senior managers. Alarmingly, a study conducted by Microsoft pointed out that almost 40 per cent of the global workforce had been planning to resign in 2021.[1]

A point to ponder here: were they leaving the job or the harsh conditions and selfish leaders who did not know how to manage them? Could they be faulted for not wanting to continue, when they were mistreated and not allowed to fulfil their potential? Why was it expected that they would perform or think like leaders and be inspired to contribute, serve the customers, and treat the organization as their own when their needs were not met?

Naturally, they could not continue in those conditions, and this resulted in a shortage of labour in many sectors. Workers finally took a stand against low wages, which had not kept up with the spiralling cost of living. Why should they have struggled with zero benefits and no job security,

---

[1] Penn, Rick, and Eric Nezamis, 'Job Openings and Quits Reach Record Highs in 2021, Layoffs and Discharges Fall to Record Lows', *Monthly Labor Review*, June 2022, https://tinyurl.com/ycmrayjv. Accessed on 10 June 2024; Microsoft, *2021 Work Trend Index: Annual Report: The Next Great Disruption Is Hybrid Work – Are We Ready?*, 22 March 2021, https://tinyurl.com/mrxwa27e. Accessed on 27 May 2024.

and for what? To make their rich employers wealthier? What is worse, some workers were not allowed to meet their basic human needs, like personal hygiene or reasonable lunch breaks, and were expected to work during natural disasters like tornados. For instance, as per an *NBC News* report, six Amazon workers at a distribution centre lost their lives during a tornado in Edwardsville, Illinois, raising questions regarding the company's emergency preparations.[2]

This is not restricted to the US alone. In Japan, workers are questioning the culture of *karoshi*, which literally means working till death. It glorifies overwork, working overtime, and maintaining a punishing schedule, discouraging the existence of a personal life (which is considered a distraction). The Japanese and other Asian youth have retaliated by subscribing to the *tang ping* concept, or the desire to lie flat, which rejects the pressure of the contemporary style of management and living a purely materialistic life chasing goals like marriage, property ownership, etc.

Similarly, there is pushback against China's infamous 996 formula, another example of a brutal business culture that encourages a 12-hour workday, from 9.00 a.m. to 9.00 p.m., six days a week, which can and does adversely impact worker health and well-being.

Meanwhile, South Korean workers protested for better conditions, job security, and fair wages, after receiving little support from the government during the pandemic. The year

---

[2] Farivar, Cyrus, and Zoe Schiffer, 'Amazon Worker Deaths in Tornados Raise Questions about Tornado Training and Cellphone Policy', *NBC News*, 15 December 2021, https://tinyurl.com/3umcmkv9. Accessed on 27 May 2024.

2021 saw thousands of workers of the Korean Confederation of Trade Unions (KCTU) protesting, with many dressed in costumes from the Netflix show *Squid Game* to showcase the plight of temporary and contract-based employees who had suffered the most.[3]

These examples of protests and demands for change highlight the growing backlash against the distortion in the traditional employer–employee dynamic across the world.

Even India, the home of Karm Yoga, appears to have forgotten its ancient roots and offers a raw deal to its workers. The pitiable condition of migrant and temporary workers, who form a sizeable proportion of the economy, was evident during the lockdown in 2020. The whole country witnessed them walk for thousands of kilometres to get home when a sudden lockdown was announced. They received poor support and hardly any benefits from their employers or the government.

Tragically, their condition was not much better during employment. Most had no job security, benefits, or medical support; some were not permitted to even sit during the length of the workday, a rule that seems like a relic of the ancient past and unthinkable in today's times. This was rectified as recently as 2021, when the Tamil Nadu government introduced an amendment bill to the Tamil Nadu Shops and Establishments Act, 1947, to mandate the management to respect the employees' right to sit. A similar bill was passed in Kerala in 2018.

---

[3]Cha, Sangmi, 'Seoul Files Complaint against Unionists Who Rallied in "Squid Game" Costume', *Reuters*, 21 October 2021,
https://tinyurl.com/2cz4uxyx. Accessed on 27 May 2024.

Managers needing a government order to allow their workers to sit during work hours is shocking indeed. This speaks volumes of the harsh conditions common across many industries.

Unsurprisingly, according to a report by the Azim Premji University, 230 million Indians fell into poverty due to the pandemic, which is defined as having $1.9 per day.[4] What's more, the gap between the haves and the have-nots increased, with a continued loss of livelihoods and decreased savings.

The corporate sector does not fare better and lags behind in affecting change. I believe that it still recognizes success or leadership potential on the basis of gender, caste, or ethnicity, and not on objective parameters like quality of output, innovation, productivity, etc.

When the Covid-19 pandemic gripped the world in 2020 and the workplace shifted online, it added to the list of existing challenges. While all hell was breaking loose outside, inside the virtual office everyone was still expected to function like nothing had changed. But long lockdowns, increased isolation, growing stress levels, and an absence of avenues of recreation or wellness took a toll on the physical and mental health of aspiring and current leaders. And this is apart from the usual gamut of infrastructural, social, political, and climate change problems, which have made the modern workplace, and in turn the personal lives of the employees, challenging.

---

[4]Centre for Sustainable Employment, Azim Premji University, *State of Working India 2021: One Year of Covid-19*, 2021, https://tinyurl.com/26tn3uan. Accessed on 10 June 2024.

Suffice to say, the contemporary model of leadership and doing business is unsustainable—it has placed undue pressure on natural and human resources and has not allowed people to live or work with purpose, joy, and dignity. It has nurtured an unbalanced ecosystem that views employees not as individuals with aspirations, but as an indistinguishable group from whom work needs to be extracted at any cost.

Everyone is aware of these problems, so the question remains: why does the system still continue with its obvious flaws? It's not that no one wants to change. Leaders are the first to seek change; but they want to change the world, and not their own mindset towards the work, the organization, and their people.

Relationship with Work at an Individual Level: It's Complicated

Yes, the overall relationship of employers and employees is complex, but so is the personal relationship that leaders or employees have with themselves and their work. The challenges at the macro level are many and these are compounded by their insufficient understanding of how they should manage themselves.

Work is obviously critical as a source of income but few approach it with joy. Who has not heard or used the term 'Monday blues'? Employees are upset at the mere idea of office at the beginning of the week; they perceive work to be a chore and a source of stress, anger, anxiety, and grief. How can such employees become thought leaders and game changers, delight customers, or bring about change? If they dislike their role, lack creativity, and have no motivation to perform or improve, how will they add value and grow?

Some who desire growth are unable to access opportunities and resources available to other sections of the population due to systemic issues like caste, race, gender, etc., and face disillusionment and stagnation. At the same time, there are others who are able to climb the proverbial corporate ladder and achieve their basic goals, but are driven by factors like competitiveness, desire, materialism, ego, and greed. They want to succeed, without caring about the means to do so. In this quest for personal glory, great power, and wealth, they face conflicts at work and in life.

Some of them toil night and day on this journey; the term 'workaholics' has been coined in their honour, and most of them are proud to be called so. Just like an alcoholic is driven to drink, the workaholic is driven to work compulsively. They are almost robotic in their existence, spending their waking hours consumed by ever-changing goals. They are not aware that any act, even if it is a duty, is unhealthy when it becomes an obsession or compulsion. Such leaders or workers have no hobbies, personal life, or satisfaction, and consequently no joy. They suffer from assorted health and family problems and do not believe their approach is deeply flawed. This is obviously the wrong relationship to have with one's duty and household or workplace.

If workaholism is flawed, then so is not investing the right amount of effort. Too much leisure time leaves the worker disinterested and dissatisfied, and has negative consequences for their growth and that of their organization.

Thus, it is common to see a significant portion of the workforce either overly attached to or poorly engaged with their customer, team, work, or business. What adds to the challenge is the different forms of mistreatment, harassment, or discrimination they face at the hands of their ineffective leaders.

Here are some real-life examples to illustrate micro-aggressions and biases that reduce engagement and foster discontent at the workplace (names withheld on request):

- I remember in the early stages of my career, I would sit for lunch with a friend who was a senior assistant. After a few days of observing this, a well-meaning senior manager approached me with the sincere advice that I should avoid this practice, as it would harm my 'image' and lead to me being perceived as an assistant and not as a potential manager; that is, it would affect my chances of growth. I never understood this 'us vs them' line of thought and am still in touch with the friend, more than a decade after leaving the organization. But this is a common illustration of the thought process of the management. They look down upon the less powerful members of their department or team, although the latter are the ones who invest long hours to ensure things run smoothly. Can we imagine the impact this had on the assistant who used to look up to the said manager? This kind of discriminatory behaviour eventually reveals itself in the form of lower pay, poor benefits, and (in)direct forms of harassment.
- A few years ago, a friend had applied for a full-time job after half a decade of working from home (she had been raising her child). The company replied to her that her total experience was insufficient for

the role, as she had not been working from office. They wanted to subtract those years of working from home from her CV. As if the location of the work could magically improve or diminish its quality or importance. The human resource manager offered her a much lower salary than her male counterparts with similar experience. Naturally, she refused the offer. But it begs the question: should one's work not amount to anything merely based on the location or gender? This is a clear example of gender-based discrimination that prevents women leaders from coming back into the workforce and demotivates employees in the ecosystem.

- A colleague once mentioned that he was praised by his superior for working long hours even in the midst of a transfer. He later confessed that he was staying back for the complimentary evening snack that he wanted to enjoy along with the free Internet and air conditioning, which had not yet been installed at home. Meanwhile, his friend who left on time after completing all the deliverables was called a 'half-day worker' and not considered dedicated, as he enjoyed 'other interests outside the office', clearly an unimaginable offence. Can we imagine the impact this would have had on his level of engagement, when his contribution was devalued for such a flimsy reason?

These may appear to be small incidents but they have a big impact on the morale, mindset, health, and engagement levels of the concerned employees and on the professional landscape itself.

Why is morale and wellness considered valuable?

Because being truly *swasth*, both mentally and physically, is a key responsibility to the self. Indian medical tradition considers the mind and body to be one. The Hindi word *swasth* means 'healthy', and is etymologically defined as *apne mein sthit* or 'being situated within'. So being healthy is not about achieving a size-zero figure or big biceps, but about being one with the self and the higher Self, and about the integration of all the layers and organs of the body.

Without that, one cannot hope to think right, act boldly, or take on challenging assignments. An exhausted mind–body can never work to the best of its ability and will set one up for disaster. A rope may appear as a snake to a disturbed mind and a molehill bigger than a mountain.

If an individual cannot take care of their own health, how will they take care of their loved ones or the health of their team? If they set a wrong example and ignore the responsibility to themselves in terms of health or any other aspect, they may unwittingly influence others to do the same.

Let us begin with mental health. In society or at the workplace, it is generally considered a weakness to take time off for one's mental well-being. Mental health is not believed to be critical or 'real' enough to affect success or the bottom line. The common belief is that if one complains of burnout, mental turmoil, or extreme fatigue, it is an excuse to shirk work and they just need to 'shake it off'.

But Karm Yoga inspires one to manage mental health on a day-to-day basis and not as an afterthought. It focusses on understanding and managing the mind to improve the response to external stimuli.

> *udharedatman aatmaanam naatmanam avasadayet*
> *atmaiva hyatmano bandhur atmaiv ripuratmanaha*

(Bhagavad Gita 6:5)

That is, the mind can be a friend and also an enemy of the self, so one must take care of it and befriend it.

How does the mind behave? It comes under the control of the gunas and reacts with guilt, greed, anger, and stress by worrying, avoiding introspection, and indulging whenever possible. The modern culture of binge drinking on weekends and binge watching OTT platforms is an example of this nature of indulgence.

Even though the brain knows that these actions are harmful in the long run, it is unable to stop the mind from exerting its will. It is stubborn and supports itself with logic and long-winded explanations. For example, justifying greed as a reward for achieving a goal, which further results in binge shopping and hoarding, justifying anger through blame games, and so on, is the mind's way of allowing itself to behave as it wants. A lot of effort is required to manage and discipline it. The mind avoids that effort and chooses the easy route of giving in to the emotion that is the most dominant at the time.

Many people aspiring for success are not aware of how to manage their minds and do not invest time or effort in taking care of their emotions. They may spend hours grooming the external self but do not spend even a few minutes to tend to the needs of the mind. Consider this: don't they go to great lengths to take care of their smartphone or laptop? Then why can they not invest the same effort in taking care of the mind? Is it not more valuable than the phone? Should they not prevent it from getting scratched, that is, not let it get anxious, upset, stressed, or disturbed? It is not replaceable, so there is all the more reason to do so.

Or consider another example. There is a stream of dirty water flowing outside a house. Will the owner not go to great lengths to prevent it from flowing in? Will they accept the garbage of another person, however close their relationship with them might be? Then why should they accept negativity, stress, insecurity, or anger from another? They should not, but sometimes they do, both at home and at the workplace.

When a senior or a colleague does not appreciate or promote these individuals, it affects their self-worth. This is natural, but why should they let it demotivate or demoralize them for a long time? They should be open to accepting positive feedback, but not if it is in the form of malicious comments, harassment, and gossip. Why can't they refuse to be affected by them, and block them in the same way they block the stream of dirty water? If they believe what the rest of the world says and do not have faith in their own potential, how will others? They need to be aware of their skills and talent, irrespective of the opinion of others. Yes, it is natural to have self-doubt, but it can be conquered with hard work, detachment, and practice.

In the Gita, we see that when Lord Krishna explained to Arjuna how one can manage the mind, the latter was overcome with doubt and said, 'The mind is restless, strong and willful. How can I control it? It may be easier to control the wind.' (Bhagavad Gita 6:34)

Lord Krishna replied:

asanshyama mahabaho mano durnigraham chalam
abhyasena tu kaunteya vairagyena cha grihyate

(Bhagavad Gita 6:35)

That is, 'undoubtedly Arjuna, it is difficult to control the mind, but it can be done with practice and detachment.'

A Personal Example of Managing the Mind: How I Managed My Imposter Syndrome

Many years ago, during an internship at a well-known financial organization, I realized I suffered from something called imposter syndrome, which makes one doubt their skills, talent, and achievements. At the workplace, outwardly I was calm and confident, but internally it felt like I was putting on a performance that would soon become evident to all.

Every organization has its fair share of problems and mine was not any different, but my challenges were compounded by the syndrome. It was not easy to accept it, but I was operating from a space of ego, fear, and doubt, and didn't know it at the time. I did not have faith in my work, potential, and abilities. This made me focus overly on the opinion of others, filled me with worry about the future, and led me to squander opportunities that would have enhanced my performance. It was not nice being overwhelmed all the time because the role was interesting and allowed me to grow. But fitting in was a challenge, and so was managing the self and the work.

Tired of being tired, I made a conscious decision to change and started searching for new ways to refine my thought process. Reading and implementing the teachings of Karm Yoga helped me change my mindset. It allowed me to manage stress, perform with the right attitude, and stop worrying about the results, as these were factors outside my control.

It taught me that the causes of stress will always exist, so one cannot wish them away but only hope to manage them. I began to manage stress with regular pranayama and yoga. Other times, I pretended to be confident (although it was far from the truth) and continued till I really believed it.

As I became more self-assured, it became easier to manage the responsibilities, collaborate with colleagues, and take on independent projects. It was still difficult and I took it one day at a time. But with determined practice, steady progress was made. The 7 Lessons helped reassure me, so did learning about the gunas, desire management, the *yagya*s (compulsory duties), and the importance of identity. The support of my family and friends was also invaluable; I don't think I would have succeeded in managing the stress without their guidance.

Of course, there are still moments and days of self-doubt; they come and go, but they do not overwhelm me or stop me from pursuing my goals like they used to. For instance, it took me 10 years to start work on my first book, but just a few months to begin the second one. Doesn't this qualify as progress? And if I can do it, so can anyone else. What or who was holding me back? Only my mind and my ignorance, not the world.

Whatever your goal may be—to learn a new language, start a business, improve financial literacy, or to care for the family—if it is dutiful, it is purposeful. It can be achieved with the mindset of Karm Yoga.

The Pandemic's Impact on Mental Health

The general and personal examples discussed above highlight the fact that the mind can be brought under control for a successful and pleasant work-life. Thankfully, the conversation on this crucial subject is gaining ground in the post-pandemic economy.

It is better late than never, as cases of depression rose in 2020 by 53.2 million globally (a 27.6 per cent rise above pre-pandemic levels), and cases of anxiety rose by 76.2 million (a 25.6 per cent rise), as per a study published in *The Lancet*.[5]

This is why many organizations that did not offer support for mental health pre-pandemic are doing so today, and have also started offering resources to cope with these unprecedented times. For instance, a Bengaluru-based start-up, which specializes in data-driven transformation for companies across industries, offered yoga and mental health consultation sessions to employees battling pandemic stress. It also provided a Covid-19 helpline during the second and third waves to offer support for medical consultations, expense reimbursement, hospital admissions, etc.

Accenture, a multinational organization specializing in information technology services and consulting, introduced an assistance programme to offer counselling services to its employees and their families. It also offered grief counselling sessions and a mental health portal to provide

---

[5] COVID-19 Mental Disorders Collaborators, 'Global Prevalence and Burden of Depressive and Anxiety Disorders in 204 Countries and Territories in 2020 due to the COVID-19 Pandemic', *The Lancet*, Vol. 398, No. 10312, 2021, pp. 1700–12, https://tinyurl.com/4w236wdw. Accessed on 27 May 2024.

support during the pandemic. In 2021, it had more than 1,600 mental health advocates offering support throughout the organization.[6]

ITC Hotels boosted morale by connecting with its employees with the help of its human resources team. Each manager was connected with a minimum of 10 employees and was responsible for their and their family's well-being on a daily basis.[7]

These were welcome karm yogic corporate initiatives. At a personal level, managing wellness on a regular basis can be achieved by following a *dinacharya* or a cycle of activities as per Ayurveda, the ancient Indian science of complete wellness. It offers a structure to the workday, while emphasizing that a break from the routine is also essential to refresh the mind. This is why hobbies, regular breaks, holidays, weekend trips, etc., are critical to the process of recharging the self.

Also, many influential personalities like tennis world champion Naomi Osaka and Olympian Simone Biles, amongst others, have become vocal about their struggles with mental health and inspired the world to listen. When they opted out of major competitions like the 2021 French Open and the 2020 Olympics, respectively, they shone the spotlight on the importance of taking care of the self. They had trained their entire lives to compete at the highest level but realized that their participation could not come without a cost, which they

---

[6]'Return to the Workplace', *accenture*, https://tinyurl.com/y5eum3c7. Accessed on 12 August 2024.

[7]'ITC Hotels Prioritizes Employees Safety and Well-being; Rolls Out Several Activities to Engage Them', *hotelier india*, 29 April 2020, https://tinyurl.com/3fnw44n6. Accessed on 12 August 2024.

were not ready to pay. It underlined the fact that success must be meaningful and not come at the expense of everything else. They continue to inspire millions to take care of their mental health and reject the stigma attached to it.

Hopefully, this renewed focus on overall wellness will continue in the future as well. And maybe the next time one feels burnt out or overwhelmed, they will be emboldened to seek the necessary support, which their ecosystem will be able to provide.

Making It Work: The Advent of the Hybrid System

Indeed, we need a better way to work and think, and to manage and lead. As mentioned earlier, the pandemic underlined this need for change and accelerated the introduction of new workplace models, technologies, processes, and systems. The most transformative one was the rise of the work from home (WFH) concept and the hybrid work phenomenon, which had hitherto faced resistance.

This came with its own challenges like unending Zoom calls, poor audio and video quality in meetings, and fatigue, but it also encouraged flexibility, brought in work–life balance, enhanced motivation, and offered freedom from location constraints without compromising on productivity. It allowed businesses to attract and retain a diverse pool of talent that had hitherto not been accessible to them. It also encouraged women leaders and people with disabilities, along with other groups who are usually sidelined, to participate in greater numbers.

However, the blurring of boundaries between work and home also increased stress and led to burnout, exhaustion, anxiety, and sleeplessness. This was further aggravated by multiple lockdowns, social isolation, Covid-19, and delayed payments or salary cuts. The good news, though, is that many companies and governments are waking up to the importance of flexibility and adopting measures to support their employees.

In India, many companies have continued to introduce programmes and activities focussed on enhanced reskilling opportunities, flexible employment terms, motivation-building exercises, team welfare, counselling, and recruitment from Tier-2 cities like Chandigarh, Kochi, Indore, Coimbatore, and Trivandrum, amongst others.

One such company is Hindustan Unilever (HUL), the country's largest fast-moving consumer goods company, which introduced two flexible work models for employees and gig workers. The U-Work scheme, also offered globally by its parent company, offered flexibility along with retirement and medical benefits, and the Open2U model offered gig workers financial and medical benefits.[8]

Ajay Ganesh, formerly the senior human resources manager at SunEdison, India's premier solar company offering end-to-end renewable energy solutions, shared what the company did to motivate their employees: 'We ensured all our employees became "green partners", allowing them to earn a certain percentage of the rewards from the leads generated and sales closed. Plus, we paid the full salaries on time and there were no defaults even when the times were tough.'[9]

---

[8] 'HUL Offers Flexible Working Options for Employees, Gig Workers: Report', *Business Standard*, 10 December 2021, https://tinyurl.com/yh4hy44w. Accessed on 27 May 2024.
[9] Conveyed personally to the author.

Priya Vivek, co-founder and head of revenue and partnerships at the start-up Qoruz, a tech platform in the influencer marketing space, shared the steps they took to improve morale: 'We ensured paid leave for those afflicted with Covid and for those who needed it for personal reasons. We offered work from home and vaccine reimbursements for all employees. We also surprised the team with small gifts, cakes for birthdays or work anniversaries, and planned small activities to keep them motivated.'[10]

These were inspiring karm yogi actions because they demonstrated that the businesses cared for the well-being of their employees, who are at the heart and soul of operations. Can one imagine the engagement and motivation level of employees at the places that offered no support, and perhaps gave pay cuts? Those may have been regular business decisions, but they surely needed to be handled in a humane and sensitive manner. Businesses should certainly not be inspired by Better.com, a digital mortgage lender, whose founder Vishal Garg sacked 900 employees over a Zoom call, right before the start of the holiday season in the US. Naturally, this act went viral on social media and demonstrated poor judgement and a lack of empathy, values that are necessary for a leadership position.[11]

Sometimes when businesses behave questionably, governments step in and protect the employees. To

---

[10] Conveyed personally to the author.
[11] '"Shocking and Devastating." 3000 People at Better.com Get the Sack After Vishal Garg Returns as CEO, Staff Reveal They Get No Communication', *The Economic Times*, 10 March 2022, https://tinyurl.com/3njupbvn. Accessed on 12 August 2024.

streamline the WFH culture, the Portuguese government mandated in 2021 that employers could not message or call their teams after work hours without paying stiff penalties. They also disallowed them from monitoring their productivity when working from home and struck down the need to have face-to-face meetings. Countries like the UAE, Belgium, New Zealand, and Iceland, amongst others, are experimenting with a shorter four-day work-week to ensure a more productive and happier workforce. Whichever system continues must factor in the wellness of the people it engages.

Holistic Wellness: Health as a Duty to the Self

Along with mental well-being, one aspiring for success must ensure physical fitness, which is a key aspect of self-management.

The practice of Hatha Yoga is recommended for holistic wellness. It is an ancient system of physical exercise which includes pranayama (management of the life force) and yoga asanas or poses. It can be combined with a healthy diet, meditation, mindfulness, natural living, and a good sleep routine for maximum benefit.

Pranayama

Pran is the life force within and is symbolized by the breath, and *ayama* means 'to control'; thus pranayama is the management of the life force itself and not just a mere breathing exercise. It is an ancient yet highly effective practice that ensures free flow of energy within the body, while its blockage causes diseases. When the pran is strong, the mind is calm, the intellect sharp, and the body disease-free. It is said that if the mind is disturbed, the breathing becomes shallow; and if the breathing becomes shallow, the mind becomes stressed. To bring it into equilibrium, a series of breathing exercises like *kapalbhati* (or the breath of fire), *bhastrika* (forceful inhalation and exhalation), *anulom vilom* (alternate nostril breathing), etc., are suggested in various proportions. They must be practised in the recommended way under the supervision of a guru or teacher.

apane juhvati pranam prane panam tathapare
pran apanagati ruddhva pranayama parayanah
apare niyataharah pranan praneshu juhvati

(Bhagavad Gita 4:29–30)

That is, the one who desires self-empowerment must practise the system of pranayama and control their intake of food to manage the mind and the senses.

Yoga Asanas

Yoga asanas are a series of poses that, combined with hand *mudra*s or gestures, are designed to bring the mind–body under control. Each finger represents a different element within the body—the thumb represents fire, the index finger represents air, the middle finger space, the ring finger earth, and the little finger water. Folding the fingers in different mudras creates gestures that are said to balance these five elements and the body.

The myriad benefits of asanas are well-known and they must be practised regularly to increase concentration and manage stress, and for complete wellness. During the pandemic, even schools and colleges, including my son's school, conducted yoga classes to facilitate an easy return to the offline system of education. Through this, they supported the physical and mental well-being of the young minds as they navigated the challenges thrown up by those unprecedented times.

Knowledge: A Protective Barrier

With or without a pandemic, the causes of mental and physical stress will always exist. It is up to the student, the leader, the householder, and the worker to add a layer of knowledge and detachment to insulate themselves against these causes.

My grandfather used the process of cutting a jackfruit to explain this to my sister and me, back when we were learning the Gita from him. He would say that when you cut a jackfruit, your hand will get stained with its milk. But if you apply a layer of coconut oil to your hands, the milk will not stick and they will remain clean. What changed? The jackfruit, the milk, and the hand remained the same, but the barrier of oil added in the second instance protected the hand. The practice of yoga, meditation, and mudras are such layers that we must apply to protect and heal during difficult times.

How I Practise the Self-Management Principles

The importance of these self-management principles inspired me to continue my yoga asana practice while working on this book.

Initially, I had planned to take a break from the practice to free up a chunk of time for writing in the morning. But that would have meant months of no practice, which was not a pleasant option. Plus, I had to practise what I was suggesting to others! So I continued with it even though I was tempted to skip on many days. I further boosted my morning routine by offering gratitude and practising pranayama along with hand mudras.

These are simple actions but can go a long way to boost productivity. They help me feel calm, positive, and grounded; only after I finish them do I plan the day with a to-do list (in a task and goals journal), and then I perform the tasks as per the order of importance. Sattva-guna is the highest in the morning; that is when I handle the most important tasks. It helps to master the morning; and if we can do that, there is no reason why we won't be able to make the entire day productive, then the week, and so on.

Want to try a simple pranayama? In the morning, sit in a quiet place on a mat with your back straight and eyes closed. Breathe in for one count, hold for four counts, exhale for two counts, and let the breath remain outside for two counts. Increase the proportion slowly after a few days, if possible. Then, breathe in for two counts, hold for eight, exhale for four, and let it stay out for four. Practise a few rounds and savour the calming effect.

Moderation and Balance: The Middle Path

Going ahead, another key element of the mindset management system is balance and moderation. This is one of the main teachings of Lord Gautama Buddha, the founder of Buddhism. He advised all to 'follow the middle path', which is to neither suffer, eat, sleep, or indulge excessively, nor starve or punish the self.

The Gita explains this further:

> *yuktahara viharasya yukta chestasya karmasu*
> *yukta swapnavabodhasya yogo bhavati dukhha*

(Bhagavad Gita 6:17)

This clarifies that everything needs to be in moderation and regulated with yoga, whether food, recreation, work, or sleep. One aspiring for success must not overeat, as too much food is difficult to digest; or eat too little, as that causes nutritional deficiencies. Strict and long fasts are a big no-no as well.

Similarly, the individual must not indulge excessively, as that disturbs the mental equilibrium, or have only a few avenues of recreation, as that leads to burnout. They must not oversleep, as it will make them lazy; nor skimp on sleep, as that will make them sick. And they must not overwork to the point of becoming a workaholic, nor invest the minimum possible effort, as that will not allow them to achieve their goals.

Thus, they must choose wisely, be it work, leisure, food, sleep, or any other aspect of life. Whether they choose moderation or indulgence, yagya or adharma (the wrong way of living), or Karm Yoga or materialism—these choices will determine whether they succeed.

If they choose sattva-guna, the unselfish kaam, or the good desire, and a life of moderation, they will succeed in bringing synergy and elevation in thought and action. It will empower and free them from the whirlwind of emotions, which is the defining feature of modern existence.

The Three Key Shaktis or Energies: Working in Sync

Karm Yoga's stress on holistic self-management, with mental and physical wellness measures and an attitude of moderation, nurtures the three main energies or *shakti*s that are present in all beings:

1. **Ichha shakti:** It is the willpower needed to achieve one's goals. It helps one perform with an indomitable spirit and clear focus.
2. **Gyan shakti:** It is the power and curiosity to learn. It helps one strive for knowledge and excellence, so that they can contribute effectively at home and the workplace.
3. **Kriya shakti:** It is the power to implement the knowledge, realize one's vision, and fructify one's plans.

Let's examine how these can be utilized to achieve one's goals in the workplace.

If a team member wants to reach their monthly or annual sales target, they must have the desire or plan (*ichha*) to do so, the knowledge (gyan) to do it, and the physical ability (*kriya*) to execute it. They need to have a firm grasp on the strategy and align it with the vision and mission of the organization. Further, they must be clear about the strategic target in terms of the value or volume they want to achieve, the existing wholesale/retail/online network, and the role of other team members. If the latter are highly motivated, they can be a wonderful resource to support them. But if their knowledge does not support their plan, then it is worthless to the individual.

The saying 'if we do not know where we have to go, any road will take us there' refers to the kind of situation that must be avoided. If team members don't have knowledge of their product, sales force, market, or the dealers, they will not be able to implement the plan even if it is clearly defined. Similarly, if they have big goals and deep knowledge but are demotivated, they will not be able to get their plan off the ground. The competition will come up with a better product/service and the company will begin to lose customers.

KEY TAKEAWAYS

- Mental and physical fitness are prerequisites to Karm Yoga.
- Mental health management is for all.
- One has to manage oneself first and then the family or team.
- The mind can be purified with yoga, pranayama, meditation, and mudras.
- The tenets of Karm Yoga ensure success and self-realization.

3

Understanding One's Role in Society

Compulsory Social Duties or Obligations

*om poornamadah poornamidam
poornaat poornamudachyate
poornasya poornamaaday poornameva vashishyate*

[That is complete, this is complete, from completeness comes the completeness. If completeness is taken from it, completeness remains.]

—Shanti Path from Isha Upanishad

After understanding what initiates work, the management of the gunas, and how to manage the health, let's focus on the next aspect of preparing oneself for the path of Karm Yoga: discharging one's social obligations.

Karm Yoga inspires one to discharge the obligations towards society in the spirit of sacrifice or yagya, which is a promise, a belief, and an act of personal discipline that elevates a simple action to the level of elevated karm. It is not the mere act of placing offerings into the holy fire, a ritualistic affair, but a mindset that ensures material, spiritual, and social growth, leading to *moksha-prapti* or liberation.

In ancient times, practising yagyas was obligatory and advisable for all, as it was believed the world originated from them:

*saha yagyah prajah srishtva purovacha prajapatih
anena prasavishyadhvam esha vo stvishta kama dhuk*

(Bhagavad Gita 3:10)

That is, when the world was created, the Higher Power stated that humans were blessed with yagyas that would help them achieve all they desired.

A yagya entails performing the compulsory as well as occupational duties for something bigger than selfish pleasure—a higher purpose. However, a higher purpose does not imply that one must forsake goals or not care for one's personal or financial needs. Or that one must renounce the world and move to a forest. How would one be able to succeed by doing that? It would probably make one realize that it is more difficult to live in harmony with everyone in the family and the community than to live alone in the forest.

Embracing a purpose and a yagya spirit is to live life to the fullest within the norms of society. It is to work, earn, and contribute by walking on the path of Karm Yoga till the very end, as without earning how can one help others? Essentially, it involves performing one's duty without exception.

Depending on one's age, personality, and lifestyle, there are varied prescribed sacrifices for different sections of society. A student, a single worker, and the householder must perform different yagyas to ensure success at their respective stage.

For example, a student's yagya is education; they must focus on learning, which is a form of sacrifice called gyan yagya. After some years, they may be encouraged to perform a ritual called vivaha yagya or marriage, and enter the next stage of life—namely the *grihastha* or householder stage. Their yagya here is to take care of the family and to treat them with love and respect. This is progress from *brahmacharya* (celibacy or student life) to a controlled form of indulgence.

In the pandemic era, a good example of a yagya was performing one's duty even in difficult situations. During the lockdowns, the workers, medical staff, and frontline employees remained dedicated to meeting the needs of the common people in the spirit of yagya. As countries shut down and people sheltered at home for months, they performed their duty. It was not merely for financial reasons, and most were not paid any additional amount, even though simply showing up was an act of bravery. They did not abandon their work despite the grave risks posed to them and their families. This elevated their actions to the higher level of karm by removing selfish reasons like fame, wealth, or ego. This selflessness and courage in the face of danger was real leadership and an example of yagya in action.

Thus, broadly, any act that is a duty, is unselfish, engages the intellect, does not involve indulgence, and elevates the doer is a yagya.

Why Should One Choose a Life of Yagya?

Working with discipline, success, and purpose can transform one's life into a yagya. One aspiring for financial and spiritual success will choose to live and work in a higher dimension to ensure that their success is both meaningful and sustainable.

For Meaningful Success

The principles of Karm Yoga say that one's success is meaningful only if everyone else is successful too. The mantra of the pandemic—'Only if everyone is safe can the individual be safe'—is in line with the ancient Indian philosophy that believes 'everyone's well-being is my well-being'. Surprisingly, it took a global pandemic to demonstrate this, but it is still better late than never. During the pandemic, no country was safe if the virus was active in a corner of the world.

Similarly, in an organization, if only the CEO is thriving and receiving accolades along with large pay cheques, while others in the team are barely recognized and struggle to eke out a living, can they or their company be termed successful? If the employees cannot meet their basic needs, how will they be inspired to work? How long can this type of situation continue? Apparently for long, as this practice seems fairly common. But it is a clear source of future problems. It signals that the contribution of management is disproportionately valuable compared to that of the worker. Differences in compensation are to be expected, but the gap must not be so vast that it threatens the workers' survival. And surely, it must not be based on gender, age, ethnicity, orientation, or caste, something that happens often enough.

For Sustainable Success

Most people want success that can be replicated again and again. The philosophy of Karm Yoga encourages them to achieve it in a sustainable way without harming the concerned stakeholders. Why? Because it considers living and working for selfish reasons a sin.

Doesn't nature function in the spirit of yagya? The sun and the moon serve all living beings equally and their unselfish existence is yoga and yagya in action. Surya or the Sun God was regarded as one of the most important karm yogis in the scriptures, as his actions ensured life on Earth. Similarly, the stars serve the universe; they do not enjoy their own light. Nor do the rivers and lakes drink their water. Their unselfish karm was highlighted in ancient texts in order to offer respect to nature. So why shouldn't we function in the same way, when we are also a part of nature?

> *evam pravartitam chakram nanuvartayatihah yah*
> *aghayur indriyaramo mogham partha sa jivati*
>
> (Bhagavad Gita 3:16)

That is, one who does not live by the cycle of sacrifice leads a life of sin, as such an individual only exists for gratifying their senses.

Ladder of Growth: Interconnected Relationship

Using the Ladder of Growth, one can further understand the intersection of the yagyas, nature, comprehensive duties (karms), the doers, and the Higher Power, and their importance.

The Ladder of Growth depicting this is as follows:

- Akshar
- Brahma
- Karm
- Yagya
- Parjanya
- Bhuta
- Anna

Its bottom rung is occupied by *anna* or food, which does not just refer to wheat, grains, food, etc., but includes moonlight, sunlight, the sky, and wind—anything that nourishes the being. Next come the *bhuta*s, which are the five essential elements present in creation, including earth, air, water, fire, and the sky. This is followed by the *parjanya* or the living beings that benefit from the creation of the five bhutas and anna. The middle rung is occupied by yagya and above it is karm, followed by Brahma or scriptures and Akshar, the limitless one.

annad bhavanti bhutani parjanyad anna sambhavah
yagyad bhavati parjanyo yagyah karma samudbhavah

(Bhagavad Gita 3:14)

That is, living beings need grains, which are produced from rains. Rains come from the performance of yagyas, which in turn are a result of performing the duty.

The Gita states that duties are created by the Higher Power who also created nature. Performing them in the spirit of yagya will allow beings to continue to evolve with purpose-driven actions. This will reveal their inherent limitless potential and their pure essence, and ensure self-actualization and the realization of Brahma, the Higher Power.

Imbibing the concept of the Ladder of Growth, one aspiring for success must attempt to nurture the yagya spirit of sustainability. But what happens when one chooses not to do so?

When a Business Chooses a Non-Yagya Spirit

Today, many individuals and businesses do not work in the spirit of yagya; they are ego-driven, selfish, highly individualistic, and greedy. They do not believe in sustainable or equitable success, rather they seek unending wealth and power, and disregard the price others will have to pay for their actions. They believe in taking more, either from nature or from people, and not giving back much or at all. This should not be allowed to continue, as the world's resources are under tremendous pressure and sustainability is the only way forward. A few examples will illustrate the dangers they pose:

- A well-known organization sets up a factory by a river and offers employment to the residents of the neighbouring town. During the process of its operations, it generates hazardous waste that is dumped into the river without treatment. After one year, it rakes in big profits and is considered to be a top achiever in the country. Should its leaders be considered karm yogic in nature? No, because they are driven by the singular reason of profit, and ignore the devastation they are causing to the region and its people. Going ahead, when the town's main source of water turns toxic, will they begin to care? The leaders may consider themselves intelligent by not investing in a safe method of waste disposal, which is a big cost-saver. But when they, their employees, and their families fall sick or are unable to attend work and incur sizeable medical bills, the true cost of their operations will become evident. How many such similar companies has one read about? Many in current times for sure.

- Now let's take a real-life example. The infamous Bhopal gas tragedy of 1984 involved a poisonous leak at Union Carbide India Limited's pesticide factory in Bhopal, India. It was allegedly caused due to negligence, malfunctioning systems, and a disregard of safety procedures, which killed more than 3,000 workers and affected lakhs of others in the city. There is still no justice for the victims after 37 years—neither were they offered adequate compensation, nor did the guilty receive sufficient punishment for a crime this heinous. It is regarded as one of the most horrific disasters in the country's history, one that could have been averted if all concerned had performed their yagya or duty with care.

These examples illustrate what happens when one is driven by short-term profits and greed. The result is long-term and large-scale destruction. However, the selfish, non-yagya, and wasteful approach is widespread and considered normal in modern society.

Compulsory Yagyas or Duties: Mahayagyas

The tenets of Karm Yoga inspire one to avoid this non-yagya approach and adopt an elevated way of working and living. Since everything is interconnected in the universe, the tenets encourage a responsible and productive outlook with a collaborative mindset.

devan bhavayatanena te deva bhavayantu vah
parasparam bhaavayantah shreyah paramavaapsyatha

(Bhagavad Gita 3:11)

That is, when the gods are happy with the sacrifices, they will bless the beings, and when gods and beings work together, they will usher in prosperity. This can be ensured by performing the five key social duties or the Paanch Mahayagyas (along with the occupational ones) in recognition of one's responsibility to family, friends, team, customers, organization, community, the nation, and the world. These are:

1. Dev yagya to the Higher Power
2. Rishi yagya to sages
3. Pitra yagya to ancestors
4. Bhuta yagya to the earth
5. Manushya yagya to fellow beings

Performing them reduces the debt to the different stakeholders in the journey of empowerment. Perhaps, in modern society, there should be a credit-rating system to ensure everyone repays their debt to all the stakeholders? Of course, some debts can never be fully repaid, like the one to parents, but others can be reduced through the following:

- Prayer is a form of offering respect to a higher power with dev yagya.
- When one shares knowledge, it reduces the debt to sages and scientists who created science, language, and the like. Honouring them is rishi yagya or brahma yagya.
- When one serves one's parents, or performs the *shraadh* or holy rituals for the ancestors, one is performing the pitra yagya. Taking care of one's children and spouse is another form of honouring the sacred ancestors.
- When one plants trees or adopts a green lifestyle, one is performing the bhuta yagya.
- When one serves one's fellow beings, one is performing the manushya yagya.

One may wonder why one should owe anything to the community. Ancient Indian philosophy believed that an individual and a business were an integral part of the community and must contribute to its growth and stability. This assumes greater significance during times of upheaval and distress—an apt description for the post-pandemic, war-afflicted global economy.

The pandemic tested the Work Quotient, leadership potential, and social responsiveness of the world like never before. The true leaders were the ones who were responsive and who supported their people emotionally and financially: they discharged their yagyas or duties at a multi-stakeholder level, to the government, community, teams, and so on, without selfish intent.

Some organizations like Tata Steel offered to pay the last-drawn salary of the deceased employee till what would have been their sixtieth birthday, along with medical and residential facilities.[12] Bajaj Auto offered to pay two years' salary with a maximum limit of ₹2 lakh per month to the families of employees who died of Covid, along with an annual education allowance for their children.[13] The focus of these visionary corporates was clearly on their most important resource—the people, and not on profit.

On the other hand, there were other individuals and businesses who attempted to take the easy way out by planting stories of the work they did or the change they brought about without real groundwork. They did not care for their employees even in those most difficult of times. A manager in one such organization shared, 'Our leader did not check up on our well-being and was focussed on achieving the numbers at any cost.'[14]

The most common reason for this unevolved mindset is that such a person wrongly believes that they are 'self-made', so they owe nothing to others. But no one can become successful without the support of the community and one's people. For instance, the body is a gift from the parents, the language one speaks was created by the ancestors, the gadgets and the science one benefits from were created

---

[12] 'Tata Steel to Continue Salary for Families of Employees Who Die of Covid-19', *mint*, 25 May 2021, https://tinyurl.com/5n95jwvp. Accessed on 12 August 2024.

[13] 'Covid Drive: Bajaj Auto to Pay Salary of Deceased Staff for up to 2 Years', *CNBC TV18*, 13 May 2021, https://tinyurl.com/23tvm9sm. Accessed on 12 August 2024.

[14] Conveyed personally to the author.

by ancient and modern scientists, and the road one walks on was built by civil engineers and the labourers involved. An organization thrives thanks to its employees, vendors, and customers, amongst others; it is not a one-man army, and neither is a community. Even the sun, the air, and the bounties of nature one enjoys are boons received from a higher power.

Thus, the individual, their family, and their business enjoy a long list of contributions from others, without paying anything in return. How can they then claim their success as a personal achievement? Does it not belong to all who contributed to it?

nayam lokostyayagyasya kutonyah kurusattam

(Bhagavad Gita 4:31)

That is, without yagyas, one can never be happy in this life or the next. This is why Karm Yoga inspires one to perform the mahayagyas and acknowledge the contribution of the community. If an aspiring leader believes that they alone are fully responsible for their triumph, they are not practising Karm Yoga and cannot be considered truly successful. They can be considered a karm yogi only after they discharge their duties to their shareholders and stakeholders.

Towards the Family: Personal Yagyas

Along with the mahayagyas, one has to perform the personal yagyas, which include an individual's responsibilities towards their loved ones.

The philosophy of Karm Yoga encourages one to do so by

managing the duties at home—including logistics, nutrition, communication, and planning, amongst others—with love, joy, and care; not by commanding the family or by treating them as a vehicle for achieving selfish goals. Since one is dependent on one's family for support and vice versa, one must motivate the family to join them on the journey of empowerment. Together they can achieve so much more while performing the social and individual duties.

In fact, a parent is considered 'good' when they take care of the needs of their loved ones. Of course, the mother or father must not do so at the expense of their health (the workaholic example is relevant here as well). Sacrificing one's well-being to take care of the family is abandoning the yagya to the self (Chapter 2) and merely creates new problems.

However, even when both partners are working from office or home, it is commonly observed that the duties are not shared fairly and a much greater burden is shouldered by women. This greatly increases the pressure on them and affects their participation in other spheres of life.

During the pandemic, many women workers suffered disproportionately in terms of job/opportunity losses, reduction of income, being forced to shift to unpaid work, increased burden at home, and greater stress levels. Many were pushed out of jobs or into lower-paying ones, and fewer opportunities were available to them due to structural, safety, and social issues.

This needs to be addressed, as many studies have shown that increasing women's employment opportunities has a positive impact on the economy and on the workforce itself.

As per a World Bank report, India has one of the lowest labour force participation rates for women at less than one-third. This means that over two-thirds of Indian women aged 15 years and above do not seek work even when they are qualified. While the global participation average was 47 per cent as of 2022, the lower rate for India does not capture the unpaid work that women perform, and their involvement in labour-intensive activities is not accounted for in the formal economy.[15]

But the benefits of increasing their participation are huge. A 2018 report from McKinsey Global Institute calculated that improving gender participation in India would add $770 billion to the gross domestic product (GDP) by 2025. This is achievable by increasing the female labour force participation by just 10 percentage points, increasing the number of paid working hours, and adding more women to higher-productivity sectors.[16]

This will ensure gender-balanced teams and boardrooms, which in turn will lead to greater productivity, stability, improved quality, and higher returns on investment. The entire country will benefit when people of any gender, caste, ethnicity, or orientation—whether working at home, at the office, in the arts, in politics, or in sports—have the opportunity, support, and resources to contribute their best.

---

[15]'Working for Women in India', *World Bank Group*, 9 March 2019, https://tinyurl.com/3p85mp7b. Accessed on 10 June 2024; 'The Gender Gap in Employment: What's Holding Women Back?', *International Labour Organization*, February 2022, https://tinyurl.com/nkfzyyry. Accessed on 11 June 2024.

[16]McKinsey Global Institute, *The Power of Parity: Advancing Women's Equality in Asia Pacific*, April 2018, https://tinyurl.com/5xe4a49c. Accessed on 28 May 2024.

Towards the Shareholders, Team, Organization, and Customers: Workplace Yagyas

Next come the workplace yagyas, which include discharging one's duty and offering respect and support to the team in order to achieve group goals.

In a leadership role one is answerable to shareholders in terms of growth, good returns on investment and profitability, and future plans that must be ethical in nature.

Towards the Team

The individual must take the responsibility of their team's overall well-being. They must not view them as workhorses from whom every drop of effort needs to be squeezed out, but as individual powerhouses of talent with different needs, goals, and aspirations.

The leader must not seek to destroy anyone's self-confidence, rather they must work hard to boost it. Thus, they must praise a team member publicly, but any attempts to correct them must be handled privately. With time management, planning, and delegation, they can ensure the team stays engaged, collaborative, and productive. They have to ensure stability and cohesion by nurturing a community-like culture within the organization.

They can manage the team in the following way:

- They must honour the ethical workers in order to set a good example for others. This will encourage the team to work with integrity.

- They must ensure free flow of communication and share constructive feedback to help team members build on their strengths.
- They must offer appropriate rebuke to the wrongdoers. This is important to enhance discipline and reduce corruption.
- They must increase the financial strength of the business through ethical action. This will enable the team to ward off attacks.
- They must be unbiased when serving justice. If there is a dispute between two parties, they must resolve it effectively.
- They must ensure that the team's salary is commensurate with experience, and the working conditions are humane and flexible.
- They must protect the company from internal and external threats.

In brief, they must master the art of management, which is essentially about how to get work done from others. They must also go higher with Karm Yoga, wherein management is the art of getting the work done with a higher purpose in mind.

Towards the Customers

The leader is answerable to customers in terms of quality and choice of products, appropriate pricing, responsiveness, service, and support. The leader must seek to understand the customers' needs, deliver quality solutions that are tailor-made for them, and serve them as best as possible in their quest to lead happier, healthier lives.

Today's customer expects the business to function like a responsible member of the community. They want to feel good while associating with it and want their choices to reflect their progressive lifestyle. If the business adopts socially conscious initiatives like eco-friendly processes, sustainable packaging, labour-friendly policies, reduction of its carbon footprint, diversity, etc., it will succeed in attracting and retaining like-minded customers.

Last but not the least are the duties towards the nation and the world (some of which are a part of the mahayagyas), which will be addressed in Leadership Lesson 5 that deals with loka sangraha or the concept of community welfare.

Karm Yoga: A Heritage that Belongs to All

In the ways mentioned in the previous sections, an aspiring leader must perform the mahayagyas, the personal yagyas, and the workplace yagyas while discharging their occupational duties.

However, a layperson may not have big goals to achieve. As such, they may wonder if Karm Yoga and its spirit of yagya is applicable to them. But when one wants to learn driving, does one think, 'I won't become a race car driver anyway, so why should I try?' No, one learns it because it will help one go from Point A to Point B. Similarly, while learning to play chess, should one worry about not being able to play like five-time World Chess Champion Magnus Carlsen? Or should one enjoy the process of learning and playing chess because it is a reward in itself?

Even though one may not aspire to become the richest or the most successful person in the country or world, they still need to lead and manage their lives and navigate the challenges of the world.

So, whether a householder, a worker, or an aspiring leader, anyone can use the teachings of Karm Yoga to grow into a better person, an innovator, a change-maker, a thinker, and a leader. It will help them achieve joy, peace, and success, the elusive work–life balance, and perhaps a higher purpose.

Does that sound difficult? Every drop makes the ocean, so one can begin with small changes on a regular basis, which will add up and ensure a momentous change in attitude, habit, and mindset. This will help them accomplish one of the most difficult of tasks—the transformation and elevation of the self.

To Sum Up Briefly

In the Introduction, the principles of Karm Yoga were used to explain the seed of work and how it leads to attachment. In Chapter 1, stress was laid on managing the self by understanding the gunas and using desire intelligently. Chapter 2 discussed how the philosophy of Karm Yoga focussed on the importance of mental and physical health, and emphasized mind management as a tool of advancement and empowerment. In Chapter 3, the interdependent relationship between the doer and the multi-stakeholder economy, necessary for ensuring meaningful success, was explained.

This preparatory knowledge helps one work and live with confidence, courage, and clarity. It gives the individual a greater appreciation of their role and responsibilities towards the self and the external world. They are now ready to perform their duty or karm.

Now, what is the mindset and the Work Quotient qualities required to become an effective karm yogi? It is the mindset nurtured by the 7 Leadership Lessons of Karm Yoga, which will be explained from Chapter 4 to Chapter 10.

> ### KEY TAKEAWAYS
> - Action performed for the greater good is yagya.
> - Yagyas ensure success and sustainability.
> - The Paanch Mahayagyas help reduce one's debt to society.
> - Personal yagyas must be performed for the family.
> - Workplace yagyas must be discharged to transform into an evolved worker.

LEADERSHIP LESSONS

4

Karm Yoga Leadership Lesson 1: Discharge all Duties

Swadharma or the Duty Mindset

The greatest glory in living lies not in never falling, but in rising every time we fall.

—Nelson Mandela

The first Leadership Lesson of Karm Yoga is to discharge all the duties that are one's swadharma; that is, to inculcate the duty mindset.

sadrisham chestate svasyah prakriter gyaanvaanapi
prakritim yaanti bhutaani nigrahah kim karishyati

(Bhagavad Gita 3:33)

That is, everyone must act as per their own nature; repressing it is pointless. The concept of swadharma can be understood through the shloka of the Aitareya Upanishad that says:

charanbai madhu vindati charantsvadu mudambaram
suryasya pasya sreemanam yo na tandrayate charan
chareyveti, chareyveti

(7:15)

That is, a honeybee moves to give honey and birds enjoy tasty fruits by movement. The sun continues to shine; therefore, one should keep moving, keep moving.

This shloka inspires us to perform our duty or swadharma in the same way a honeybee, a bird, and the sun perform theirs: without stress, without complaining, and with grace. It ends with the Sanskrit word *chareyveti*, which means constant movement. It is repeated twice to convey the importance and necessity of dedicated action in the performance of duty. Is this a fitness tip or a workout instruction? No, it is a call to perform the swadharma, one's natural duty, constantly. Swadharma does not refer to a religion, like Hinduism, Islam, or Christianity. Instead, it is an inspiration to embark on the journey of self-improvement and empowerment, by avoiding stagnation and never giving up.

One aspiring for success must keep chareyveti in mind while discharging their duties and responsibilities. They must never refuse to perform their responsibilities or hand them over to someone else; work and authority can be delegated to some extent, but not responsibility.

The key elements of swadharma are:

- It is above the rule of nature.
- It functions within the boundaries of dharma.
- It is the soul's dharma to be *trigunateet*, or to flourish beyond the three gunas. The soul is beyond sattva-guna, rajo-guna, and tamo-guna, and is *sachidananda* or pure joy. Thus, self-satisfaction and joy are one's swadharma.
- With the help of tattva gyan, or the essence of pure knowledge, one can transcend the gunas.

Examples of Swadharma

At home, a householder's swadharma is to take care of the needs of the family, raise the children, honour the parents and spouse, and provide security and affection to the loved ones. They also have to repay their debts through the Paanch Mahayagyas, which is their duty to society. Some other examples of general duties are following a healthy diet and avoiding junk food, taking care of one's mental health, clearing an exam to get admission into a good school/college, etc.

At work, a manager's swadharma is not only to perform their job-related duties but also to take care of the team. They have to guide the team in their roles, offer training and support, nurture their talent, and solve the problems that cannot be addressed at their level. The team members can climb the ladder of growth and reach the pinnacle of excellence in a role that suits them, with the right support.

For instance, a naturally ambitious, independent, and enterprising worker is well-suited to start-ups; a creative and innovative mind thrives in marketing; and a people's person excels in human resource management. Each must stay true to their passion, driven by their duty, the gunas, and their specific skill set. It does not matter what path they choose—sports or arts, a not-for-profit organization or a corporate, becoming a homemaker or setting up a start-up, or anything else. If they harness their natural abilities and do their best, they can excel and continue to progress.

For instance, gifted athletes like the late Milkha Singh, tennis player Sania Mirza, the Tokyo 2020 Summer Olympics gold-medallist javelin thrower Neeraj Chopra, and the

Paralympian shooter Avani Lekhara inspired an entire country and millions across the world by following their swadharma and striving for excellence in their respective fields.

Factors Affecting the Swadharma or the Duty Mindset

The standard and quality of the performance of swadharma is affected by many factors:

- **Karta:** It depends on the nature of the karta or doer. The karta's personality will influence the task being performed, its speed, the response of the team, the quality of the result, and so on. If they are focussed and driven, and possess a good Work Quotient, they will perform in a systematic manner. If their Work Quotient is underdeveloped, they will not be able to handle the responsibilities or challenges that come their way. Everyone will face their fair share of problems when they take up any duty, but only the one with a yogic spirit will remain focussed and resilient with equanimity. They will motivate themselves and others with their grit, whereas the one with a poor attitude will be distracted and look for excuses for their failure. If they are physically present in the office but mentally enjoying on a beach, how will they coordinate the three energies of ichha, kriya, and gyan to drive action?
- **Kaaran:** Swadharma also depends on *kaaran*, which refers to the knowledge, tools, and support needed. Without the appropriate support for the respective activity, swadharma cannot be accomplished. In ancient times, one

depended on the guru and advisers for facts, information, and guidance. Today, the new-age worker can depend on their computer/laptop, Google, their smartphone, an Internet connection, and perhaps ChatGPT or artificial intelligence for knowledge or information. Without these tools, it seems virtually impossible to get anything done nowadays. Besides these, they may need specialists who can handle specific tasks and roles, along with advanced software and bigger teams, amongst other things. Whatever support is needed, the team must have the necessary infrastructure and resources to perform their task.

- **Chesta:** Another factor affecting swadharma is the *chesta* or effort invested. One needs a mix of hard work, homework, and teamwork, as one cannot perform swadharma without them. Prayer alone is not enough for success; consistent and creative action is required to realize it. Then, the harder one works, the luckier one will become.

- **Prarabdh:** *Prarabdh* refers to destiny or the accumulated karm that has started bearing fruit. The individual must accept that they are not a victim of destiny, rather they possess free will. So, they must perform their tasks by investing sharirik tapa, which is physical effort, mansik tapa, which is mental effort, and vaachik tapa, which is the effort of the voice. These are the mahayagyas of work and they must be invested in the performance of one's swadharma. An example of vaachik tapa is being truthful in nature, but it does not give one the licence to hurt others through speech or action; one should also not let others harm the self because of it. Humility is a form of mansik tapa, but it does not mean having low self-esteem. Rather, it is about controlling one's ego. Performing sharirik tapa is to engage in hard work but does not include carrying out someone else's duty. This must be avoided, along with the *nishidh karm* or prohibited acts, like robbery, kidnapping, murder, etc.

Thus, keeping in mind these factors, the swadharma must be performed to the best of one's abilities with the support of the three tapas. However, *vikriya* or the wrong work will happen seemingly almost by itself. For example, food will go stale without outside effort; it is something that happens naturally. In the same way, knowledge and skill will deteriorate if not applied. If not enhanced, they will become redundant and outdated, and not serve their purpose.

How I Understood the Concept of Swadharma

My grandfather used to advise us to advance on the path of swadharma by putting in our best effort every day. We were not sure how to implement this. So he explained it as follows: 'You must become more *sahishnu* [a person with the ability to struggle] if you want to be *jaishnu* [a person with the ability to win].' This signifies that we should learn to struggle and toughen up, face the challenges of life, and not run away from them, if we want to succeed in following our swadharma.

Usually, we prefer to avoid the first part, becoming sahishnu, and head directly to the second part. But doing so can rob us of fundamental life lessons that are necessary for character-building and self-management. Just like a building cannot stand without a solid foundation, similarly, we cannot achieve our goals if we do not become strong enough to face whatever comes our way. If we want to perform our swadharma wholeheartedly, we have no other option but to become strong enough to face the cyclical nature of the world.

Challenges in Performing Swadharma

Practising the duty mindset is not attractive to human nature, which craves novelty, excitement, and adventure—something that the same old work cannot provide.

At home, one may find chores repetitive and uninteresting; one may avoid performing them, or engage with them joylessly and/or with disdain. This can become a habit and bring down the quality of the work, and the satisfaction one gets from performing it. For instance, when a householder is expected to host a guest they are not fond of, they will not welcome the responsibility of cooking. Will such a meal be of the highest quality? No, it won't.

On the other hand, if they are expecting close friends, they will go all out to craft a memorable evening. The meal will be prepared with patience and care. Will it not be tastier, more attractively presented, and generously offered compared to the one prepared for the first guest? Yes, but why is that so? The answer is that in the second instance, the householder performing the duty or swadharma will be doing it joyfully, even if it increases their workload. The responsibility is similar in both cases, but it is the change that will elevate the process, enhance the quality of effort invested, and transform the final result.

Similarly, at the workplace, some millennial or aspiring leaders may find their duty boring, tedious, and unfulfilling. They may perform it half-heartedly, which can affect their engagement level and bring down the quality of the product/service. They may be attracted to a colleague's duty, as it may appear interesting and different. But that is *pardharma* (the duty of another person) and they must never engage in it by abandoning their own duty. This is considered one of the biggest wrongs that can be committed in the karmic realm.

sreyan swadharmo vigunah paradharmat svanushthitat
swadharme nidhanam shreyah paradharmo bhayaawahah

(Bhagavad Gita 3:35)

That is, it is better to perform your duty incorrectly than to perform another's perfectly. A person may suffer while discharging their duty, but they should never abandon it and follow another, as that will bring ruin.

Yes, it is easy to desire another's duty, but even that will become monotonous after a period of time. The grass may appear greener on the neighbour's side, but it is the same there too. It is the intellect, overpowered by emotions, that makes it appear different.

Work and its mystical nature remain the same; it is the attitude with which work is approached that makes one consider it a punishment or a prize, a fun activity or a boring chore.

When it is considered a burden, it leads to the abandonment of duty, which has harmful consequences for all the stakeholders. For instance, a situation where a doctor loses interest in taking care of their patients can create problems for the families they are treating. Till the families are able to find a suitable replacement, they will suffer the consequences of the doctor's impulsive decision. If the number of such doctors increases, the whole community will suffer. Can one imagine the condition of the country/world if the doctors, nurses, and the support staff had evaded their duty during the pandemic?

This principle is not limited to those who offer critical services like doctors or engineers. Rather, it is applicable to each and every member of society. They must ensure they perform their duty with enthusiasm and perfection, even in the face of numerous challenges.

Root Cause of Challenges in Swadharma

Even when performing the swadharma may seem disastrous, it should still be considered unavoidable.

In the ancient Indian epic Mahabharata, on the battlefield of Kurukshetra, Pandava Prince Arjuna wondered why he should engage in a devastating war. Lord Krishna replied that He had to because it was His responsibility, His duty. Even if it led to violence, it had to be performed. Arjuna's mind was not steady and was full of doubts. His emotions had impaired his judgement, so he asked Lord Krishna, 'If the duty is so important, why do so many people not want to perform it? Rather, what is it that inspires one to do wrong things, that is, to commit sin? It is as if there is some force that is pushing one towards it, for it is not natural for anyone to desire to engage in sin.' (Bhagavad Gita 3:36)

Lord Krishna replied:

> *kaam esha krodh esha rajo-guna samudhbhavah*
> *mahashano maha papma viddhyenamiha vairinam.*

> (Bhagavad Gita 3:37)

That is, it is kaam, or desire, and anger fuelled by rajo-guna that forces one to become adharmic.

However, He also clarified and added later, 'It is not true that all desires are bad. The dharmic ones are good. Amidst all the desires, I am the dharmic one.' (Bhagavad Gita 7:11)

Thus, desire is not harmful when it is dharmic in nature and supports one in the working or householder stage. It inspires one to enjoy life and repay the debts to society, and offers security and stability. It also helps one perform the swadharma fully, which is considered higher than any other form of work, elevating not only the doer but humanity itself.

Addressing Some Common Arguments and Doubts

- **'I want to be a happy-go-lucky person and not struggle with yoga and swadharma.'** This is exactly what yoga and swadharma can help one with. Karm Yoga will help one perform the duty in the right way, without which one cannot hope to find peace or purpose. It will nurture joy and contentment, which exist within us. As long as we keep searching for them outside, we will remain anxious and unstable.
- **'Following my swadharma is boring and it will mean that I have to give up a life of desires.'** No, Karm Yoga

or swadharma does not advocate that one should give up all desires, as it is not possible to do so. The philosophy of Karm Yoga understands that forsaking desires is not as simple as taking a decision to quit them one fine day. Desires will not end suddenly, even if one suppresses them. Rather, Karm Yoga encourages the reduction of adharmic or selfish desires and their conversion into dharmic ones. It also advises one to enjoy the desires that are in line with dharma, albeit in moderation.

Work Quotient Qualities Nurtured by Lesson 1

- Self-reliance
- Hard work and commitment
- Being dutiful

> ### KEY TAKEAWAYS
> - One must discharge one's duty or swadharma to the best of one's abilities.
> - Living joyfully is also part of swadharma.
> - Performing one's swadharma ensures empowerment and nurtures joy within.
> - One needs to be sahishnu before one can become jaishnu.
> - Following swadharma helps all of humanity.

5

Karm Yoga Leadership Lesson 2: Duties Must Be Discharged with Advanced Intelligence

The Buddhi Yoga Mindset

Failure is success in progress.

—Albert Einstein

The second Leadership Lesson of Karm Yoga is that duties must be discharged with advanced intelligence, or with the Buddhi Yoga mindset.

In the previous lesson, it was discussed that one must perform swadharma. How can it be performed with excellence? Through Buddhi Yoga. Ancient Indian philosophy placed Buddhi Yoga on a high pedestal and considered it essential to achieve one's goals. Its importance was illustrated in many scriptures, couplets, and hymns—in them, one sought the boon of pure intelligence, rather than riches, fame, or power.

durena hyavaram karm buddhiyogad dhananjaya
buddhau sharanam anvichha kripanah phala hetavah

(Bhagavad Gita 2:49)

That is, action performed merely for the result is far lower than action performed in Buddhi Yoga. So, seek the grace of knowledge for success.

Thus, Buddhi Yoga is the art of imbibing pure knowledge, which is the gateway to liberation. It stresses on the control of the mind–body and the senses so that one can perform one's duties with equanimity. With discipline, stability, and the cultivation of *vivek* (the ability to discern), it can empower one's conscience and enhance the ability to manage the gunas.

Seven Stages of Intelligence

It is possible to discharge one's swadharma with excellence and innovation by progressing through the different stages of intelligence, which are:

1. **Shushrusha:** It is the emerging desire to understand a subject. A key trait, it denotes the beginning of the journey towards knowledge. Nurturing it is imperative for the one who wants to grow as a strategic thinker and a change-maker.
2. **Shravan:** It is the ability to listen carefully to what is being taught. One is a student in front of the subject-matter expert or guru, and if one wants to progress, they must learn with patience and dedication.
3. **Grahan:** It involves understanding a subject in depth so that its essence becomes clear. Incomplete knowledge is a dangerous thing, so one must attempt to understand the complete spectrum of information. One can go above and beyond it, but never fall short of what is required.
4. **Dhaaran:** It is the ability to remember what is taught.

Knowledge is of little use if it is learnt and forgotten. It must be understood and applied when required.

5. **Uhapoh:** It is to evolve the thought process and arrive at a meaningful conclusion after receiving new information. No one should blindly follow or trust a source of information in this era of fake news, deepfakes, and false data. They must wait to understand the big picture, verify the sources, and only after that share it with a larger audience.
6. **Arth vigyaan:** The next step is to implement the knowledge and not let it remain on paper. If it is not brought into action, what is its use? So-called industry experts and thought leaders who help neither others nor themselves remain so merely in name, as their knowledge becomes outdated and redundant over time.
7. **Tattva gyaan:** *Tattva* means the essence of a subject. If one knows the basis or the tattva of anything, it can be understood in its entirety. Then, even if it is presented in a different form, it will still be recognizable. For example, after understanding the nature and appearance of gold—whether it is presented in the form of a bangle, earring, necklace, or ring—one will be able to identify it as a gold ornament.

Buddhi Yoga: Wisdom at Its Best

The importance of pure knowledge, not factual information, is further illustrated in the most important mantra of the Sanatana Dharma (the eternal religion)—the Gayatri Mantra. The prayer seeks to purify one's intellect with the help of the One who takes away sorrow and nurtures joy. His blessings ensure that one receives the light of knowledge, which can drive out *agyan* or the darkness of ignorance. According to ancient Indian philosophy, the grace of the guru and the Supreme Teacher is what helps one imbibe pure knowledge.

Kabir Das, a fifteenth-century Indian mystic poet and saint, also elaborated on this:

> *guru govind dou khade, kake lagoo paye,*
> *balihari guru aapne govind diyo bataye.*

In this *doha* (couplet), when a student meets both the guru (who imparts knowledge) and Him, the student becomes conflicted as to whom they should honour first. Both are equally important to them. The guru points to God (as the guru is without ego) and God points to the guru, signifying that the teacher is akin to the Supreme Teacher. Since the guru is the route to God, the student bows to him first but not without keeping in mind the higher truth.

In the Gita, Lord Krishna advises Arjuna that once pure knowledge is imbibed, leading one to understand what is action and inaction, one can become *mukt* or free of the unfortunate. One will be blessed and receive freedom from the constant cycle of birth and rebirth. (Bhagavad Gita 4:16–7)

This signifies that pure knowledge leads to bliss, freedom, excellence, and meaningful achievement. On the other hand, *buddhi* or intelligence leads to only material success.

Buddhi Yoga vs Buddhi: What Is the Difference?

Let's understand the difference between Buddhi Yoga and buddhi with an example. An intelligent person is said to be working with their buddhi when they excel in their role as, say, doctor, teacher, writer, etc. But sometimes their intelligence can be tempted by wealth, fame, or power and take them down the wrong path. They may use their in-depth understanding of, say, the financial, banking, and taxation rules of the country to bypass them, not pay any taxes, or take huge loans without the intention of repaying them. They may then justify their actions with the rationale that they did not create the flaws in the system, they merely took advantage of them, so how can they be blamed? They may believe that they have won in the short run, as their actions will inflate their and their company's wealth. This is an example of a person who is not practising Buddhi Yoga. Rather, they are focussed on exploiting financial loopholes for personal or corporate benefit, which may harm the stakeholders and the nation's economy in the long run.

The fugitive businessman Nirav Modi, who is under investigation for a $2-billion Punjab National Bank fraud, is a case in point.[17] Similarly, there are many famous corporations and CEOs who work with buddhi and not the Buddhi Yoga mindset. They pay close to no taxes, and avoid discharging their responsibilities to the community.

As per a 2021 report by *The New York Times*, FedEx, which offers transportation, e-commerce, and business services worldwide, Nike, the world's largest athletic apparel company, and many other big corporations avoided paying tax liability for three straight years in the US.[18]

---

[17] 'What Is PNB Scam', *Business Standard*, https://tinyurl.com/4eby9hct. Accessed on 12 August 2024.

[18] Cohen, Patricia, 'No Federal Taxes for Dozens of Big, Profitable Companies', *The New York Times*, 7 October 2021, https://tinyurl.com/mr2dddkc. Accessed on 29 May 2024.

These companies are 'leaders' in their respective industries, but opted for this deeply flawed approach as a result of using the lower form of buddhi or intelligence. When such businesses pay low to zero taxes, they adversely affect investment in infrastructure, public health, research, and the social welfare projects of the nation.

If this (that is, the refusal to perform the Paanch Mahayagyas) occurs in underdeveloped countries, it will hinder the progress of the common people. It will further widen the gap between the haves and the have-nots and exacerbate social, political, and infrastructural problems. These problems are compounded when others who admire this so-called intelligent approach follow suit. This is why their numbers seem to be growing by leaps and bounds in modern times. For such CEOs and their admirers, the process of growth is not important, only the result is. They bend the rules, beat the system, and misuse the power, people, and resources at their disposal even though they are aware of the impact of their actions.

Thus, the mere presence of intellect is not enough, as it can be misled by ego, greed, hostile ambition, hatred, or anger. When it is not directed towards the greater good but is used to create problems, to foster arguments, for armchair consulting, or to harm the society, it should be considered to be of little use.

Thankfully, the Buddhi Yoga mindset has the potential to promote exemplary action and refine the contemporary social landscape, which is plagued by scams, misappropriations, frauds, etc.

Equity and Inclusion

Buddhi Yoga can also address the serious challenges caused by lack of inclusion, inequity, and discrimination on the basis of gender, race, caste, or disability.

For instance, can a leading organization that does not prefer to hire women, senior workers, or people with disabilities be deemed successful, or said to be practising Buddhi Yoga? Certainly not, although such organizations are quite common.

A colleague once shared that her manager did not want to hire young women or invest in their training because they would marry, have children, and quit the team. This thought process is so common and so wrong on multiple levels; such a manager is not even working with buddhi, let alone Buddhi Yoga. Sometimes, even after women are recruited, it is implied that they are diversity hires—that their recruitment was based solely on gender rather than on talent, experience, or skill.

A similar and strange justification is used to exclude people with disabilities or older workers, on the assumption that they will not be able to perform. How can such a company and community expect to grow? Does excluding a large part of the population demonstrate intelligence?

These managers, working with buddhi and not with a Buddhi Yoga mindset, may possess the basic knowledge required to perform their role but lack the vision to lead and nurture diverse groups of people. Even if they are a part of senior management, they should be offered sensitivity and behavioural training to ensure that they create a level playing field at the workplace.

Mistake Management: Implementing the Buddhi and Karm Yoga Mindset

The tenets of Buddhi Yoga and Karm Yoga can be used to address different types of wrongdoing, or a faulty thought process, and correct mistakes in the personal/professional space:

- To err is natural but one must attempt to identify it early on. Not identifying or accepting one's error is where problems start.
- One must avoid defending one's error by making excuses and diverting blame, or through logic, and should not justify it vis-à-vis someone else. This does not make it go away. It makes it grow bigger, and without immediate intervention it becomes unmanageable. For example, the world's largest aerospace company Boeing's culture of concealment was held responsible for the crash of two of its 737 aircraft, as per a US report.[19]
- One must fix the error systematically, instead of covering it up or complaining about it.
- One should not hesitate to ask for assistance if a mistake is made. This does not mean one is weak, rather it shows that one is aware of what is required to grow.
- One must ensure the error does not recur by introducing new processes, improving support,

---

[19] 'Boeing's "Culture of Concealment" to Blame for 737 Crashes', *BBC*, 16 September 2020, https://tinyurl.com/55w75ccd. Accessed on 10 June 2024.

enhancing communication, and offering training, amongst other things.
- If the error has occurred due to issues like rash decision-making or improper people management, one must encourage improvement through developmental efforts, workshops, training, etc.

The critical point is that a mistake must not be treated like a full stop. It is a setback, but it does not close all the roads to growth. Rather, it must be considered a learning experience to shape the future and used as a stepping stone to success.

Thus, with the Buddhi Yoga mindset, one can carve out a new path for advancement. This path prizes career longevity and success in a sustainable manner, without compromising on the family's or team's mental/physical health, dignity, and aspirations.

Addressing Some Common Arguments and Doubts

- **'Buddhi Yoga is not possible in modern society.'** One must choose to practise Buddhi Yoga if one wants to have the power to do the right thing. Self-control is freedom for such an individual because they want to achieve their goals in a sustainable manner, without abandoning their ethics.
- **'Mind–body control is very difficult.'** One has to understand that it is the mind that is in contact with the world, and it determines whether one has a positive or negative experience. If it is not managed, then a simple

situation will become difficult to bear. Rather than trying to control the world and all its minds, it is better to manage one's own mind, body, and senses. It is difficult but certainly possible with Buddhi Yoga; and it is not optional if one wants to succeed at Karm Yoga.

Work Quotient Qualities Nurtured by Lesson 2

- Empathy
- Faith
- Treating all equally

KEY TAKEAWAYS

- Practising Buddhi Yoga is superior to merely working with buddhi or intelligence.
- It ensures right action and excellence.
- It inspires a sense of calm and helps with management of the gunas.
- It ensures one's intelligence is used for a higher purpose.
- It can refine the contemporary social landscape, which faces multiple challenges.

6

Karm Yoga Leadership Lesson 3: Duties Must Be Discharged within the Framework of Yogic Action, and Treated like Worship

The Faith Mindset

Success is liking yourself, liking what you do, and liking how you do it.

—Maya Angelou

The third Karm Yoga Leadership Lesson is to discharge one's duties within the framework of yogic action. That is, in the spirit of yagya and as a divine responsibility (as explained in Chapter 3). This transforms them into a form of prayer. Isn't that much better than worshipping Him with flowers, incense, milk, and sandalwood?

mayi sarvaani karmaani sanyasyaadhyatma chetasa

(Bhagavad Gita 3:30)

That is, offer all your work to Me, by being dedicated to Me. This is the approach to work as outlined by Lord Krishna, simple yet effective.

The Framework of Yogic Action: Work Is Worship

When the individual engages with duty in the spirit of divinity, they are essentially using Karm Yoga Lesson 3, which brings together the art of work, the art of knowledge, and the art of devotion in the following way:

- **Working in Karm Yoga (action):** When one's action is of the highest quality or considered perfect, one is said to be working in Karm Yoga. On this path, one accepts the result as being proportionate to the effort invested.
- **Working in Gyan Yoga (knowledge):** When one performs with pure knowledge at the highest level, or if one's knowledge is complete, one is said to be working in Gyan Yoga. On this path, the result one receives is believed to be due to one's actions in a past life (or past lives).
- **Working in Bhakti Yoga (devoted service):** When one works to serve all, and thus the divine, one is said to be working in Bhakti Yoga. On this path, the result one receives is considered a blessing from the Higher Power.

One can note that all the three forms of yoga stress on the importance of karm or elevated work. Their interconnected nature offers a sublime path of advancement: perfect action (Karm Yoga) leads to pure knowledge (Gyan Yoga), and vice versa. Together, they nourish *bhakti* or devotion, and inspire a life of joy and purpose.

yatah pravrittir bhutaanaam yena sarvam idam tatam
swakarmana tamabhyarchya siddhim vindati maanavah

(Bhagavad Gita 18:46)

That is, through work, one can worship Him and attain success. For example, at the workplace, when an individual excels in a role supported by complete knowledge, and safeguards the interests of all the stakeholders, they are said to be using the complete framework of Karm, Gyan, and Bhakti Yoga.

A doctor or lawyer who serves their financially challenged patients pro bono, an engineer who contributes their best efforts in an underdeveloped region, a journalist who strives to bring truth to the people, and a businessman who offers reasonably priced and high-quality products that enhance the lives of their customers, are examples of people performing karm with purpose.

On the contrary, if one's knowledge is utilized merely for wealth generation for the self (and has harmful consequences for others), then even if the task is performed with intelligence, one is not engaging in Gyan Yoga. If one invests effort in the duty only to satisfy the ego or for personal glory, one is not engaging in Karm Yoga. It is a rajo-guni action. And if one's action is driven by love that is limited to the family or friends, one is not working in Bhakti Yoga.

Thus, any element of selfishness, greed, and ego brings down the quality of karm from the advanced level of yoga—be it Karm, Gyan, or Bhakti—into the lower realm of mere action.

However, if it is not possible for a beginner yogi to implement all the three forms of yoga in this framework, they can choose to begin with Karm or Bhakti Yoga, as these are considered simpler than Gyan Yoga. Karm Yoga can be the first step towards fulfilment and success; along with the support of Bhakti Yoga, the individual may make rapid progress in the pursuit of empowerment.

But what is Bhakti Yoga?

The Faith Mindset with Bhakti Yoga

When duty is performed in the spirit of bhakti or devotion, without selfish desires, and as a pure service, it transforms into Bhakti Yoga. It is perceived to be a simpler path compared to Karm or Gyan Yoga, but one can choose any route that is suitable to their personality and life goals. It does not matter whether one is engaged in Karm or Gyan Yoga, the spirit of bhakti can uplift one's actions and thoughts on either path.

Bhakti is a personal relationship between a being and the Higher Power. It is pure faith coupled with intelligent understanding; it is never blind. Rather, it is deep, meaningful, elevating, and rewarding. It is the gateway to success, and a tool to access a higher consciousness and comprehend the nature of divinity. A devotee is considered the highest amongst all the seekers in the Gita:

yoginaam api sarveshaam mad gatenaantar atmana
sradhhavaan bhajate yo maam sa me yuktatamo matah

(Bhagavad Gita 6:47)

That is, the one who has faith and renders service to Him is united in yoga with Him and is the highest of all.

Who can follow Bhakti Yoga? Anyone can become a devotee by nurturing their bhakti sincerely. Often, the individual's outlook will depend on what is missing in their life. Thus, if one aspiring for success does not have a strong role model, their bhakti will be influenced by this and they will worship Him as a father figure or mentor. If they have financial struggles, they will worship Goddess Lakshmi, the Indian goddess of wealth; and if they are looking for support, they will worship Him as a friend.

An individual can choose to worship or have faith however they prefer. But they cannot pretend to nurture devotion or use someone else's method as their own. It has to be genuine if they seek a good result. This is called sakaam bhakti (prayer for a reward or support). However, when one expects no results, and worships in an unselfish way, it is called nishkaam bhakti. It is considered higher than sakaam prayer, which in turn is better than no bhakti.

Whether the individual works with sakaam or nishkaam devotion, they will attract like-minded people who are on the same path as them. But they must be careful who they associate with. They must reject the blind followers, encourage those who question them, and nurture the ones willing to go the distance to achieve their shared goals. They must also encourage their loved ones and colleagues to develop critical and independent thinking on this path, so that they are empowered to succeed.

A blind follower is a danger to themselves and to the group, as they will perform without analysis or comprehension and execute what has been communicated. Without contemplation, they will function without intelligence and the quality of their output will be suboptimal. This is the wrong way to perform one's duty and is not advocated by the Karm Yoga philosophy.

Action Fructifies with Faith

Here is a personal example of how working with faith helped me. When I started working on my first book on the teachings of the Gita, the initial months were stressful, to say the least. I wanted to do justice to the topic but could not write more than a few sentences a day. Doubt, self-rejection, and confusion plagued me. There was no clear way forward, even after a few months of struggle. It would have been easy to quit but I genuinely believed that the book could offer solace and comfort to the reader, so I plodded on.

After a few months of doing more of the same thing, the realization dawned on me that it would take something 'extra' to achieve a breakthrough. I needed to change my thought process and approach to work.

So, every morning, I submitted my thoughts to a higher power and asked for support to nurture faith—in the work, in the self, and in the Higher Power. Slowly, there was a change in my mindset. I accepted the responsibility, focussed on the work alone, and did not try to resist the challenge. Rather, I started to relish it. After a few more months, the doubts began to wane and the words came easier. It was still hard work but the suffering, fear, and stress disappeared. The journey was now enjoyable.

As the book reached its final stages, I realized that there was no publisher or agent to handle its printing and distribution. Normally, this would have worried me, but somehow it didn't this time. I continued searching while receiving rejections and pushback. Many people questioned my choice of topic, my style of writing, and the need for the book, amongst other things. It was not easy but, to my surprise, my outlook stayed optimistic.

Finally, I found a supportive publishing house that helped my book see the light of day. I believe it was faith that inspired me to accomplish my goal (publishing the book), but to reach that stage, I first had to put in the effort to write it. Without hard work, I could not have depended on bhakti alone for success, as that would have been a tamo-guni action.

What I learnt is that we should keep working towards our goals even when they are difficult and seem impossible, and even when we do not receive support from others. We should continue to think positively and reject the false suffering and stress that our mind likes to put us through; this will help us reach the finish line.

My actions fructified with the power of bhakti. But what if you do not believe in a higher power? Then you can choose to believe in yourself and in your hard work. Have faith in your dreams and keep advancing on your chosen path.

The Concept of Identity: With Bhakti

Clearly, Bhakti Yoga has many benefits, as it helps one live and work with purpose. It also helps in understanding the self, the interconnected nature of the world, and the equality of all beings. If one aspiring for success imbibes its core message, they will understand their relative position in the community and their real identity. Their false ego will then reduce, and they will accept the world as their own and avoid wrongful actions.

What is this identity being referred to here? The example of a river will help us understand it better.

There are many rivers in the world that originate in various places and flow in different directions. Where do they end? In the oceans. They all have an end point, where they become a part of something bigger. After they merge with the ocean, if one takes a bucket of water from it, will they be able to guess which river it belongs to? Not by a cursory examination. It is all water, although initially it was named differently and identified based on its country, region, point of origin, etc.

But water does not forget its identity, even if it is in a different location. It still heads back to the ocean upon the completion of its journey. In the same way, all beings have the same core identity, although they may have different names, personalities, and lives. They have a common origin and end point, wherein they will become one with the creation and the Higher Power.

Or take the example of air. Air is all around, but in every country it has one identity. It does not become different when it crosses the border. When a potter designs a small clay pot, air is enclosed inside it. Does it lose its identity or have no recollection of its higher nature? When they make a bigger pot, more air is enclosed inside it. Whether outside or inside, in a small pot or a big one, air remains the same. Its basic nature does not change, neither does it think less or more of itself depending on the vessel containing it.

Then why can we not remember our true identity, our true nature? Air and water never forget their essence. In the same way, whether we are working in a small or big company, in the role of a community leader or as a fresher, or enjoying success or facing failure, why should we lose our sense of self-worth or morals? Why should we forget our identity depending on what we are going through at the moment?

Unity of Outlook in the Upanishads

In fact, all the three yogas (Karm, Gyan, and Bhakti), help us understand our bona fide identity.

In the Mahabharata, delivering this profound message of yoga was so critical that it could not wait. It was shared right on the battlefield of Kurukshetra, even as the two armies of the Kauravas and the Pandavas stood facing each other.

The first shloka of the ancient classic Ishavasya Upanishad explains it as follows:

*om ishavasyamidam sarvam yatkinch jagatyaam jagat
ten tyakten bhunjeethah, maa gridhah kasya swiddhanam*

That is, everything is permeated by Him, whether it is moving or unmoving in the world. The Higher Power is present in everything and He is the owner of everything, of all the work and the wealth. If we can understand His nature and our own higher nature, we will realize the limitless potential of the self and stay balanced with *pragya paraad* or true knowledge.

Practising the Faith Mindset

An aspiring karm yogi can imbibe the concepts of identity, the faith mindset, the gunas, and self-management in the following way:

- They must not regard any work as unimportant as long as it is ethical and duty-oriented.
- They must accept the duty with gratitude, and consider it a divine gift.
- They must accept the result of the duty as a *prasad*. Prasad is the food and holy offerings that remain after the completion of a yagya, and are considered equal to nectar. In Indian tradition, it cannot be refused

and must be accepted with grace. The prasad may be success or failure, but the individual must respect both.
- They must accept their potential and nurture an abundance mindset.
- They must perform without fear and without the false restrictions and limitations of the mind.
- They must reject a narrow, selfish outlook, which can cause harm to others, and accept the synergies between the individual, the business, and the society.

Working within the framework of action, knowledge, and devoted service in this way can elevate one's mindset, purify one's consciousness, and transform one's work-life into a blessing.

Addressing Some Common Arguments and Doubts

- **'Everyone wants success and wealth without sharing them. Why should I care for others by practising Bhakti or Karm Yoga?'** Karm Yoga encourages all to strive for success. It is a practical philosophy, as without goals, no one will be inspired to work. It does not ask one to give up success and ambition or to avoid fame, but to ensure that these are achieved in an ethical manner and that the fruits of success are shared with the community.
- **'I have to live in a cave or forest to practise yoga.'** No, it encourages one to work within society, to perform all the duties, and achieve one's goals. How can an individual

perform their duty in the forest, and for whom will they perform it there?

Work Quotient Qualities Nurtured by Lesson 3

- Excellence
- Knowledge
- Balance

> ### KEY TAKEAWAYS
>
> - Work is worship: The framework of yogic action combines Karm, Gyan, and Bhakti Yoga.
> - All duties belong to Him, so they must be considered divine.
> - Bhakti Yoga elevates and purifies one's attitude to work-life.
> - Karm, Gyan and Bhakti Yoga highlight one's limitless potential.
> - Karm Yoga inspires one to accept life's challenges as prasad or divine gifts.

7

Karm Yoga Leadership Lesson 4: Avoid Adharmic Actions, Increase Dharmic Actions

Dharmic vs Adharmic Mindset

Your success and happiness lie in you.

—Helen Keller

The fourth Karm Yoga Leadership Lesson is to avoid the wrong, adharmic actions and increase the good ones with a dharmic mindset.

The Evolved Legacy of Dharma

Ancient Indian philosophy offers a broad description of dharma: it is an act, belief, or philosophy that purifies the self. It is also referred to as duty or the natural way of life.

It is defined by 10 broad elements, and one may note that there is no mention of divinity or religion in them. They are: *dhriti* (patience), *shama* (equanimity), *dama* (self-control), avoiding theft, *shauch* (cleanliness of one's words, body, and mind), control of sense organs, intelligence, knowledge, truth, and freedom from anger.

Practising these 10 elements and living dutifully constitutes a life of dharma. Thus, a dharmic person is patient with their family or team members, forgives them if they make mistakes, and handles difficult situations intelligently. They maintain a high standard of hygiene for their mental and physical health through self-control and management of the gunas. It does not matter what religion, creed, or community they may belong to; if they are hard-working and driven by pure inspiration, they are said to be dutiful or dharmic in nature.

Although discharging the dharmic duties is challenging (because there may be many), they should still be performed without excuses and in a timely manner. Why is prompt action important? As a famous doha of Kabir's explains:

kaal kare so aaj kar, aaj kare so ab,
pal mein parlay hoyegi, bahuri karega kab.

That is, if one must perform a duty, instead of doing it tomorrow one should do so today or, better still, immediately. The world can end in a minute, after which it will be too late.

Thus, this doha advises one to curb the habit of procrastination, which can affect the performance of one's duty. Although many believe this habit to be driven by laziness, it has both physical and emotional roots. It may develop due to one's inability to cope with the fear of failure, confusion, perceived lack of support, or the stress of perfection that can prevent one from starting a new project or finishing a critical report on time.

Support in the form of mentorship, skilling opportunities, and training can go a long way in helping an individual perform their dharma without delay.

Nature of Adharma

On the other hand, any action that should be avoided or that can harm the self or others is called adharma. It is an act or belief that sullies the mind, soul, heart, thought, and words as it flows through the mind, the tongue, and the sense organs.

The Types of Adharma

There are many types of adharma, but they can be broadly grouped into three categories:

1. **Mental sin:** Thinking about acts that can harm others, living in fear, a poor self-image, thinking about and engaging in overindulgence, or wrong acts like gossiping, avoiding the truth, avoiding hard work, envying another person's wealth or good times, plotting to cheat, thinking negatively, or misunderstanding divinity.
2. **Voice sin:** Bitterness, rudeness, lying to avoid loss or punishment even when the truth is known, gossiping, or speaking unconnected, senseless, and irrelevant things.
3. **Body sin:** Lust, stealing, violence, or hurting someone without reason through actions.

There are many other sins in this day and age, as their nature and type keep evolving and increasing over time.

The Unsustainable Outlook of Adharma

Why is adharma a concern for humanity? Let's examine the outlook of an adharmic person.

An adharmic person is one who has a purely selfish

outlook towards work and life. Their nature is in stark contrast to that of the dharmic, *viveki*, or the sattva-guni. Consumed by tamo-guna and intense rajo-guna, they are unable to manage their desires for indulgence, temporary gain, or personal benefit, even if they harm others. This attitude makes their colleagues and family members affluent in the short term, but deeply miserable in the long run. Should their uncontrollable desire, greed, anger, and ego be projected onto others? The answer is no. They should not use their desires or rage to instil fear. Rather, they must lead by example if they are in a position of power at home or in the workplace.

Why is anger considered harmful?

krodhaad bhavati sammohah sammohaat smriti vibhramah smriti bhranshaad buddhi naasho buddhi naashaat pranashyati

(Bhagavad Gita 2:63)

That is, from anger comes delusion, and with delusion memory is distorted; this leads to a loss of intelligence, which can cause one's downfall.

Anger is thus considered one of the most harmful emotions in Indian philosophy. Since ancient times, fear and greed have been used with the concept of hell and heaven to motivate common people. They were threatened with punishment or hell if they did not perform their duties, and were bribed with dreams of heaven if they lived with integrity.

This combination of fear and greed prevented most from abandoning their duty and ensured balance in society. But the ego of the extremely adharmic leaders cannot be controlled easily, as they remain unconcerned about heaven or hell. That, however, has consequences.

The Consequence of the Adharmic Mindset

Often, we may find adharmic people at the helm of affairs, be it in the business world or in the political arena. What are the consequences of their actions on themselves, their families, and the community?

Let's take the example of the Kaurava clan in Mahabharata, which explains the consequences of adharma. When their cousins, the Pandavas, who had lost the kingdom to them, returned from exile, Duryodhana, the rajsik Kaurava leader, refused to return it. The Pandavas asked for five villages in exchange. Duryodhana replied, 'I will not even give you an area of land as small as the tip of a needle.'

He allowed his adharmic nature, ego, hostile ambition, greed, and uncontrollable desire for power to cloud his judgement. Surprisingly, he was supported by many of his family members and other leaders, who didn't advise him to follow the righteous path. He did not live up to the promise of returning what was not his, which is adharma in action.

What happened as a result? A bloody war was foisted upon the kingdom, many lives were lost in the process, and the entire adharmic Kaurava clan was destroyed. With dharma on their side, the Pandavas fought for their rights on the battlefield of Kurukshetra and were victorious. Upon assuming the throne, they ushered in an era of progress, prosperity, and peace.

One may wonder why Lord Krishna, who was guiding the Pandavas, did not advocate for forgiveness, as it is a key element of dharma.

> *yada yada hi dharmasya glanir bhavati bharata*
> *abhyutthanam adharmasya tadatmaanam srijamyaham*

> (Bhagavad Gita 4:7)

Lord Krishna declared here that whenever dharma was in danger, He would come to save the good and destroy the evil. Yes, forgiveness is indeed considered important, but it is recommended for mistakes and petty crimes at a personal level. Not for crimes of a grave nature, like usurping a kingdom by fraudulent means, or violence against women and children. Forgiving these would be construed as a lapse in the justice system and allow crime to flourish.

Thus, Lord Krishna suggested war as the last resort, when all other methods of reconciliation had failed. It was aimed at removing adharma and served as a deterrent to existing/future adharmic leaders who might destabilize society and harm common people through crime, war, economic ruin, destruction, and death.

Implement and Review: Dharma vs Adharma

You can check whether or not you are practising dharma and Karm Yoga in a simple way.

- **Working with a dharmic mindset:** If you are driven by dharma or a higher purpose, you will perform your duty with a strong Work Quotient and avoid excessive indulgence in desires. You will nurture the desires that are important for the householder stage of life and fulfil ambitions in an elevated manner. Infused with sattva-guna and vivek, your actions will elevate the self

and the community through the performance of the Paanch Mahayagyas.
- **Working with an adharmic mindset:** If you are driven by narrow or hostile goals, you will be filled with *kaamna* (selfish desire), *krodh* (anger), greed, and fear. Harmful ambition, lack of ethics, ego, and lust—which are symbolic of adharma—will drive your actions to further degrade your mind. You will shirk your duties or perform them with a flawed attitude—that is, without a higher purpose. The end result will be a life of struggle, anger, fear, insecurity, and instability.

The Swirl of Sensory Pleasures

In Chapters 1 and 2, we observed that work was driven by desire and influenced by the gunas. While engaged in duty and driven by desire, what does one seek? Whether pursuing the goals of arth, kaam, dharma, or moksha, one wants the end result to bring joy in life. This is understandable, as being joyful is one's basic nature. But what happens when it becomes all-consuming?

For instance, one may constantly wish for delicious fare to satisfy the taste buds, for a partner to fall in love with, or to acquire the latest smartphone or laptop in the market (which is a status symbol). That is, their desire to gratify their senses may be unending.

Upon acquiring the love or the desired object, they may hope to enjoy its various attributes; and that does happen for a certain period of time, till one becomes bored or loses interest and needs another object to take its place. This leads to a break-up or loss/rejection of the older object of desire, and it becomes a cause of sorrow and anger for the individual.

This is true for one's occupation as well. An individual may switch jobs in search of the perfect organization or the ideal role. They may hope for the new workplace to satisfy them creatively and offer them financial stability. Initially, all will go well, and they may be joyful for some time—till a disappointment, an unhelpful colleague, or an unexpected challenge is encountered. Unable to handle these, they may prefer to quit and move on to the next place. The same cycle will then repeat on loop.

It is said that an employee leaves mainly on account of poor leadership. But what about the serial quitter or the one who is often disappointed? Such a person is on an eternal quest for true joy but rarely finds it. They seek that one person, object, or workplace that can offer pure joy, but all of these fall short of their expectations, which are sky high. Everywhere they go, they find novel problems to complain about and novel challenges that are too difficult to face.

This is not to discourage employee turnover; it is often high in environments where harassment, discrimination, abuse, or unfair practices exist, and that is justified. But for other businesses and relationships, one needs to realize that there is no single material thing that can offer unending satisfaction. If an individual cannot find the right fit at any place or with any person, it is probably due to a poor attitude and/or a skill mismatch.

So what should they do?

> *ye hi sansparsha ja bhoga duhkha yonaya eva te*
> *aadyantavantah kaunteya na teshu ramate budhah*

(Bhagavad Gita 5:22)

That is, an intelligent person must stay away from those pleasures that have an end and a beginning, as they are sources of sorrow. They should, thus, disallow temporary objects from controlling their happiness.

Think about it. Gadgets, cryptocurrency, wealth, fame, or other assets—their nature is temporary. When the world is changing constantly, how can they stay stationary and offer permanent happiness and security? They cannot, and this is why depending on them for emotional support is foolhardy. It is not that one should not enjoy their presence, but one should not become dependent on them, or their absence will lead to dissatisfaction and instability.

Similarly, depending on external factors for approval is dangerous. For instance, some workers seek validation from their industry or colleagues, which is natural to some extent. When they receive praise from a supervisor or colleague, they are on top of the world. When the same person criticizes them, they are completely dejected. The presence of these extreme reactions disturbs their mind; but why do they give another the power to control their emotions in the first place? Is that wise? It only makes them dependent on the other, without knowing whether the other has their best interests at heart.

A similar thing happened with me, and helped me understand this concept better. When I took a break from full-time office work after my son was born, there were many well-wishers and relatives who remarked that I was wasting my education by sitting at home. But after 10 months, when I joined a new place, the same people pointed out that my decision was wrong again and that I would neglect my duties towards my son. Their conflicting stance did sting at the time, as I was unsure of the way ahead. I questioned my decision both times and struggled with the pros and cons, worried that I would have less time with my son, or that I wouldn't be able to do justice to the role. But why did I need validation from other people? Why did I let them question my decision?

Well, it was not easy to stay unaffected, as young mothers, or aspiring leaders for that matter, are constantly offered conflicting advice. It can be a confusing time, as most of us are learning on the job, be it motherhood or a managerial position. At that time, I believed it was the right thing to do for me and my family, and so I went ahead with my decision. Luckily, it worked out for us. But even if it had been a mistake, it would have been mine to make and learn from.

Thus, what I want to share is that we should not let the words or actions of others influence our destiny. If we seek approval, constant validation, or joy from them, it will distract us from our growth and journey. How will we build our confidence if we do not believe in our decisions? And how will others have faith in us if we don't have faith in ourselves?

This is not to say that one should not listen to the advice of a few trusted sources; that is important, no doubt. But for all others, we must thank them politely for their interest and continue to think independently, make informed decisions, and learn from our experiences.

Fostering Contentment and Vivek

The intelligence or ability to think independently and separate the right from the wrong is called vivek. It can empower one to understand that depending on material assets or external validation is self-defeating.

If one's nature is highly rajsik or tamsik, the vivek becomes weak and does not help one make the right decision. Such a person will not be satisfied with any acquisition, partner, or position, whoever or whatever it may be. They will prefer to blame other people and things for their discontent or sorrow. When they become overly attached to material things or people, they will receive constant shocks once they start losing them, as they all have an end point—be it a fluctuating stock portfolio, falling cryptocurrency, or the loss of an expensive watch. If they seek pleasure in indulgences like gambling or smoking, they may enjoy them initially but as they are addictive in nature, they can and will trouble them later. The more they indulge in such addictions, the less satisfied they will become, eventually leading to health, work, and family problems.

On the other hand, a sattvik person has a strong vivek, and is able to understand that the contentment and joy they get from transitory things or habits is fleeting and false, and that these will make them insecure in the long run. Vivek helps them understand the unstable nature of the material world and improves their emotional ability to deal with it. It inspires them to learn about the eternal nature of the spiritual world, which prevents them from embarking on an endless and frustrating journey, desperately searching for security, success, or happiness. The different forms of yoga can also help them understand that their contentment should come from performing their duty, and not from the results or the factors associated with it.

This does not mean that they must abandon the sources of joy in their life, or not nurture any ambition or goals. It signifies that they must reduce harmful indulgence, selfish ambition, and unnecessary desires, and maintain a good attitude towards the fruit of their actions. If it does not meet their expectations, they should not be dejected but should put in the required effort to acquire their desired result in the future.

However, one cannot manage the self or change one's outlook by reading up on Karm Yoga, vivek, contentment, or pure knowledge. These sense organs are not easy to control; they will find something, some person or object, to get attached to. They will push one to seek joy, novelty, and excessive indulgence, and distract from their duty.

One aspiring for success can practise a viveki attitude by ensuring the following:

- Always perform the duty or *kartavya*.
- Work hard—without laziness, without excuses or complaints, and with dedication.
- Find satisfaction in the duty (not in indulgence) by believing it is important, irrespective of its nature or the quantum of work.
- Actively reject *akartavya* or non-duty.
- Learn to say 'no' to the self and to others with vivek, and stand up for the self and the family or team.
- Have faith in the self's potential and wait for success with a positive attitude.
- Increase the dharmic responsibilities and reduce adharmic actions.

I believe in seeking the *kripa* (grace) of the following powers to nurture vivek, especially while embarking on a new initiative, or when facing a challenge (like attempting to reduce indulgence):

- **Ishwar kripa (the blessing of the Higher Power):** Seeking His support reduces ego and inspires us to never give up.
- **Guru kripa (the support of the teacher):** It makes us aware that our knowledge is not complete, so it reduces pride and inspires us to seek the support of experts and gurus.
- **Shastra kripa (the opportunity to study and learn more):** It instils respect for the instruments or technical tools needed to perform one's duty, like computers, machines, gadgets, etc.
- **Atma kripa (the strength of self-confidence):** It instils respect for the self and work ethic. If we cannot respect ourselves, how will we revere the work, family, and team members, and how will others respect us?

In this way, you can strive to strengthen the viveki mindset in the pursuit of dharmic duties and abandon the non-viveki or non-discerning attitude.

Addressing Some Common Arguments and Doubts

- **'I don't need dharma, so why would I need Karm Yoga?'** Even if one does not want dharma, one may still want to live in peace and prosperity. For that, one must strive for freedom from poor habits, negative emotions, and an immature mindset, which may hamper one's growth. One need not belong to a particular religion to follow any form of yoga or dharma, as it is a universal truth. One can simply follow the 10 tenets of dharma to lead an elevated life.
- **'What is a higher goal: wealth or fame?'** Wealth is

considered to be at the lowest rung of desires. A higher goal is to strive for wealth along with fame. Above them is the desire for fame; it is considered significant, as it helps one achieve a high status in society. If one desires fame, one must ensure that they earn it in an honourable way or by using skill, not by false pretenses. A mix of wealth and fame is considered valuable, as both ensure the financial stability and welfare of the family and the organization.

Work Quotient Qualities Nurtured by Lesson 4

- Discipline and stability
- Integrity and ethics
- Innovation

KEY TAKEAWAYS

- Working with dharmic desires is better than working with selfish ones.
- All desire is not wrong, otherwise no act would ever be performed.
- Increasing dharmic activities reaps rich dividends in the long run.
- Adharma leads to devastation and ruin.
- One must remain alert whether one is working with a dharmic or adharmic mindset.

8

Karm Yoga Leadership Lesson 5: Increase Duties that Lead to Community Welfare

Loka Sangraha Mindset

Be the change you wish to see in the world.

—Mahatma Gandhi

The fifth Leadership Lesson of Karm Yoga is loka sangraha, or the concept of community or overall welfare.

By now, one is familiar with the first four lessons of Karm Yoga:

1. Swadharma
2. Buddhi Yoga
3. Using the framework of Gyan, Karm, and Bhakti Yoga
4. Performing dharma and reducing adharma

For whom does one practise these lessons? Primarily, for one's own benefit and that of loved ones. But to advance to the next stage of Karm Yoga, one needs to broaden the outlook and include a larger purpose—the spirit of loka sangraha. It includes the performance of duties with inclusiveness, without selfishness, and for the welfare of all.

*labhante brahmanirvanam rishayah kshina kalmashah
chhinna dvaidha yataatmaanah sarvabhuta hite rataah*

(Bhagavad Gita 5:25)

That is, one who is beyond doubt, has the mind under control, and works for the welfare of others will be the one to achieve liberation. Loka sangraha includes the following, but is not restricted to these alone:

- Creating a larger vision for the self and for the community/nation, which includes all stakeholders.
- Improving the awareness of people regarding better ways of working with Karm Yoga and loka sangraha.
- Introducing processes, infrastructure, systems, and practices to support transformation in line with the larger vision. For example, if a community's vision is to support diversity, it must create the necessary infrastructure and policies for it. It cannot merely pay lip service to, say, gender equality; it must ensure equal pay, safe working conditions, maternity leave, and childcare support services, amongst other things. It must ensure that women are not relegated to the 'mommy' or the slow track. Thus, in order to offer true support, it is not only the infrastructure and policies that must be changed but also the mindset.
- Encouraging the public–private partnership model to create large-scale impact. A real-life example is the association of HUL, HSBC India, and Brihanmumbai Municipal Corporation to set up a Suvidha Centre in

Dharavi, home to one of the largest slums in Asia. This is an act of loka sangraha, as the community centre aims to support government efforts in offering safe water and sanitation facilities at an affordable cost. This is a welcome karm yogi move designed to raise the standard of living of those who need it the most.
- Engaging with community representatives and civil society to explore avenues of participation, such as providing sports scholarships, art and culture patronage, charitable initiatives, nation-building activities, medical welfare programmes, etc.

Thus, the loka sangraha mindset aims to remove the false dichotomies between the individual and community, business and community, workers and management, and collective and individual consciousness.

It is an extension of the yogic thought process that says: 'My welfare is everyone's and everyone's welfare is mine.' This is much needed today, as one cannot be considered truly successful if large sections of the community are left behind and wealth/power is concentrated in the hands of a few. This is why everyone must devote time, effort, talent, and financial resources towards these activities, not for selfish gain, but with a genuine interest.

The concept of *vasudhaiva kutumbakam*—viewing the whole world as one's own village—from the Maha Upanishad explains this mindset further. It implies social welfare is everyone's responsibility, and that it is incumbent upon all to assume it.

Impact of Loka Sangraha: Thought-Provoking and Action-Oriented Mindset

The loka sangraha mindset inspires one to perform ethical and elevated actions for the common good, which in turn may inspire others to follow suit.

karmanaiv hi sansiddhimaasthitaa janakaadayah
lokasangraham evapi sampashyankartumarhasi

(Bhagavad Gita 3:20)

That is, kings like Janaka, the king of Videha who was famed for his spiritual nature, became *siddha*, or experienced self-realization, by performing their duties. In the same way, one should work for the benefit of inspiring others.

Aren't Instagram and social media influencers able to connect with and influence millions of their followers? When a famous influencer uploads a reel (short video) with specific dance steps, they inspire hundreds and thousands of others to make similar ones. So why can't an aspiring thought leader with a loka sangraha mindset influence the community and workplace through their words, actions, and overall behaviour? Surely they can.

They can be the one to introduce new standards and better practices, and also the one to discourage selfish ambition with exemplary action. But this is easier said than done. It is not as simple as reading about it and implementing it the next day. Most people aspiring for success and fame engage in social responsibilities because they expect accolades, rewards, and perhaps positive press coverage. Will they continue to do so in the absence of cameras?

Karm Yoga states that if one performs a noble deed and expects recognition for it, it is not wrong. One should still encourage oneself, as it is better than doing a harmful deed.

na buddhi bhedam janayed agyanam karma sanginaam
joshayet sarva karmaani vidvaan yuktah samaacharan

(Bhagavad Gita 3:26)

That is, an intelligent person should not stop one who is working in an incorrect manner, but lead them by example.

Karm Yoga advises one to eventually strive to perform their duty even if there is no reward or recognition. Is that likely? Yes, it is possible that after years or decades of performing in the spirit of righteousness, one may experience a shift in perspective and experience spiritual growth. Such an individual may then be inspired to imbibe the spirit of real loka sangraha, and that should be the goal of the one aspiring for success. Till then, they can continue to perform with a sakaam mindset. Thus, Karm Yoga inspires one to not only elevate the act but also the attitude with which the act is performed.

What if One's Role Model Is Incorrect?

What if one strays from the higher path and indulges in, say, corruption and exploitation? This will have a big impact on society because, just like Instagram influencers, that individual can influence a large number of people.

yadyad aacharati sreshtas tattad evetaro janah
sa yat pramaanam kurute lokas tad anuvartate

(Bhagavad Gita 3:21)

That is, what a respectable person does, the common person follows. The world will follow the standards set by the former, so they must be careful.

The reverse is true as well. For instance, when a CEO engages in workplace sexual harassment or discriminates against certain employees, it emboldens others in the organization to behave in a similar manner and to justify the abuse and harassment as the norm. Since corporate culture starts from the top and flows downward, without a positive role model for the rest to emulate, bullying and mistreatment on the basis of gender, orientation, age, ethnicity, etc., become a part of the cost and process of doing business. Instead of loka sangraha, it eventually leads to community destruction. This is what we are witnessing in many a contemporary society and workplace; we need not look into a crystal ball to see the future.

A real-life example of a poor role model was the erstwhile head of Fox News, Roger Ailes. He was a much sought-after political consultant and a successful communications professional, responsible for making the network a household name. But he fostered a culture of misogyny and exploitation by targeting his women employees, and was accused of sexual harassment by more than 20 women. Finally, he was forced to resign in 2016.[20]

Many such leaders exist today who continue to misuse their position and power. Who is responsible for initiating change in such a scenario?

---

[20]Dockterman, Eliana, 'The True Story behind *Bombshell* and the Fox News Sexual Harassment Scandal', *Time*, 16 December 2019, https://tinyurl.com/2s9jfk8v. Accessed on 12 August 2024.

Leading Change through Loka Sangraha: Work as an Agent of Transformation

The responsibility of initiating change does not lie just with the avatars or divine reincarnations who descend upon Earth to save the good from adharma, or with the CEO or a few elected representatives working in silos. The task of community- and nation-building and contributing to the global/national economy is too complex and vast to be left to one or two people. It needs the contribution of many bold change-makers and pioneering thought leaders, from the business world, the government, and civil society. In fact, it is the responsibility of each and every person, householder, and worker to strive for positive change. A group of aspiring leaders working together can be extremely effective at bringing about large-scale change.

No wonder, then, that many great leaders like Sardar Vallabhbhai Patel and Indira Gandhi utilized the message of loka sangraha to revitalize the masses and to unlock their potential:

- Sardar Vallabhbhai Patel served as the first deputy prime minister of India from 1947 to 1950. Known as the Iron Man of the country, he is a fine example of a karm yogi leader as he was dedicated to the welfare of the nation, which is loka sangraha in action. As a participant in the Indian independence movement, he adopted the concept of *satyagraha* and the policy of non-violence propagated by Mahatma Gandhi, and demonstrated a dharmic mindset. Due to his untiring efforts, almost all the princely states were integrated into newly independent India. This demonstrated an application of Buddhi Yoga and an abhokta, akarta attitude, driven not by personal benefit but by a greater purpose.

- Indira Gandhi was the first woman prime minister of India who served from 1966 to 1977 and again from 1980 to 1984. She was committed to the welfare of the common man, which is the hallmark of a true karm yogi leader. Her visionary policies included poverty reduction programmes, nationalization initiatives, encouraging scientific research, and the development of the space programme. These were actions carried out in loka sangraha, as they were designed to make the nation self-reliant. Further, to ensure stability and peace in South Asia, she undertook the courageous decision of supporting the liberation struggle of East Pakistan, which demonstrated Buddhi Yoga in action. Under her bold leadership, India won the 1971 India–Pakistan War, leading to the creation of Bangladesh.

These two examples illustrate the loka sangraha mindset in action and demonstrate how it was used by political leaders to empower the common man.

Surprisingly, even though we in India had a pioneering woman prime minister like Mrs Gandhi decades ago, the mindset of a few regarding the potential of women leaders still remains in the Stone Age. I'm sharing a personal example to illustrate this point.

We once had an interesting discussion at a former workplace, where a male colleague casually remarked that women could not assume global or higher leadership positions as they did not possess the necessary traits. He pointed to a lack of diversity in top management positions, boardrooms, politics, and world affairs as proof of this so-called fact. He received ample support for this viewpoint from other male colleagues.

A small group of female colleagues refuted his argument in the following way. We mentioned that while growing up, women face many challenges like the lack of educational opportunities, poor nutrition, social conditioning, lack of safety, and other systemic issues. The ones who make it to the employment stage are pushed out in a few years in the name of marriage, caregiving, pregnancy, their husbands being transferred, the lack of family support, etc. Thus, the pool becomes small by the time it reaches the top. Even this group faces discrimination and bias, hitting the glass ceiling, as they are not considered a natural fit for leadership positions. It becomes a vicious cycle—their absence is taken as proof of their lack of interest or potential, and because there are just a few of them, their numbers are not enough to disprove this myth, and so it continues.

The male colleague grudgingly accepted it as a supply-chain issue, but clearly there is a complex intermingling of social, cultural, political, infrastructural, and systemic factors at play here.

Today, there are many successful women business leaders across the world, like Indra Nooyi, former chairperson and CEO of PepsiCo, Sheryl Sandberg, ex-COO of Meta Platforms, Mary Barra, CEO of General Motors, Falguni Nayar, founder of e-commerce site Nykaa, and many more, who have shown what it means to lead by example, irrespective of gender or nationality.

Yes, attitudes are evolving, but growth is slow. According to consulting and auditing company Deloitte, women held only 18.3 per cent of board seats in 2023, an increase of 4.5 per cent from the 2018 edition of the same report. Globally, women hold 23.3 per cent seats (as of 2023), and this is expected to continue along the same lines for many more years.[21]

Unfortunately, the underlying biases remain, and hurt the growth of businesses and communities who can benefit from diverse and inclusive teams. I believe that such teams have an enhanced focus on equity and the greater good, which is much needed in the post-pandemic economy. Loka sangraha will be more successful if all genders are allowed to contribute and participate to the best of their abilities.

Business, Its Leaders, and Work: As a Force for Good

Society needs the equitable attitude, higher intent, evolved vision, and service of many with a loka sangraha mindset, irrespective of gender, caste, race, or orientation. A similar message is elaborated upon in the Upanishads, which inspire one to selflessly serve the others.

One who understands the Higher Power as the cause of causes will accept that He is the one who has assigned the duties, which cannot be delegated and must be discharged for the common good. For instance, the Sun sustains life on Earth, the Moon shines at night, and the rivers continue

---

[21]Deloitte Insights, *Women in the Boardroom: A Global Perspective, 8th Edition*, 2024, https://tinyurl.com/dnsdped8. Accessed on 11 June 2024.

to flow; they never abandon their duties and continue to perform unselfishly, inspiring all to work in the same spirit.

Challenges in this Journey

Implementing loka sangraha requires abandoning harmful ambition or selfish intent for the greater good, which is difficult for many of us. To a certain extent, it is possible to put the needs of others—for instance, those of the family—before one's own, and many do succeed at it. (This is separate from prioritizing self-care or mindset management as addressed in Chapter 2.) But placing the needs of the community, team, or country ahead of one's own is challenging.

For example, the pandemic was a good opportunity for world leaders to practise loka sangraha. Instead, they practised vaccine nationalism by hoarding billions of doses of precious vaccines for their countries. This left the underdeveloped nations to fend for themselves. The result? It allowed the virus to mutate and come back in a highly infectious form, affecting both developed and underdeveloped countries. Thus, in the long run, selfish and short-sighted leadership caused trouble not only for them but also for the world.

Another challenge is that if a person attempts to work in the loka sangraha spirit, they may not receive the support of their family, community, or country. The family may worry that the individual's focus will shift to supporting other people or projects, and away from their own financial stability and responsibility. Therefore, working unselfishly with a higher purpose for loka sangraha demands a price that one needs to be ready to pay, in terms of time, money, effort, resources, talent, etc.

Many organizations do succeed in doing so. For instance, the Dallas-based Qentelli, a leading end-to-end digital transformation service company that is changing the way businesses connect through the digital medium, used their technology to give back to society when it needed it the most.

Sanjay Jupudi, president of Qentelli, shared, 'Apart from a vaccination drive for our employees in the Hyderabad office and supporting the employees who were struggling with medical expenses, we wanted to do something more. So we collected spare CPAP and BiPAP machines and with technical intervention repurposed them into non-invasive ventilators.'[22] This was a welcome karm yogi action; it supported rural hospitals in India and other developing countries, and saved many lives during the dreaded second wave of the pandemic.

Implementing the Loka Sangraha Mindset: Better Together

Indeed, loka sangraha can be a powerful tool for social transformation, but one needs to proceed with caution, as one cannot force others to change. Transformation is a slow process at a personal level, and even more so at the corporate, social, community, and national level. It cannot be brought about overnight, and certainly not by force. It will succeed only if the masses trust the one who is bringing it in, and if they see a personal benefit in it. If they suspect a hidden agenda, they will reject it even if it is beneficial to

---

[22] Conveyed personally to the author.

them. Everyone will not change instantly, but a few may; and that is a step in the right direction, which is better than none at all.

If one can demonstrate the benefits of loka sangraha to people, they may become amenable to a new way of working. One must:

- create and share one's vision on the path to a larger consciousness;
- demonstrate with words and action that one does not value profit above every other metric of success, and accept overall welfare as one's core value;
- engage with government representatives, community delegates, and other business leaders to chalk out one's vision, and collaborate with other teams and leaders to implement it;
- practise one's vision of not exploiting resources and personnel, not only in the home country but in other countries as well;
- reject lucrative plans and projects that can harm the community in the long run, and stay committed to an equitable future with sustainable models and efficient practices;
- not participate in loka sangraha with an intent to improve public relations or as a brand-building exercise, but view it as a solemn duty, without using it as a form of one-upmanship or competition (which is an inferior method of working); and
- proactively come up with new ideas, novel initiatives and programmes to give back to the community and the nation.

The spirit and actions of loka sangraha ensure that one becomes successful in the true sense of the word; one will 'have it all' because one is ready to 'do it all' for the benefit of the multi-stakeholder economy.

When individuals and businesses start functioning in this evolved manner, they will reduce harmful ambition, support one another, and meet the needs of customers and community. This will ensure prosperity and harmony in society and transform the nation into a karm yogic one.

Addressing Some Common Arguments and Doubts

- **'Loka sangraha or Karm Yoga is only about being a good person, which I already am. Will I too have to pay a price if I am engaged in dutiful work?'** Karm Yoga is not to be confused with just being a good person. It is about a transformation of the individual and the collective mindset. It empowers one with knowledge to take the necessary yet tough decisions. For example, Mahatma Gandhi, who is considered one of the finest human beings in history, had a difficult relationship with two of his elder sons. Since he dedicated his life to the cause of Indian independence, his family life was affected, but he continued to stay resolute on his path. Thus, following the path of Karm Yoga involves paying a price, in terms of time, money, effort, resources, and the like, which everyone may not be ready to do.
- **'I do not want to be successful/a leader/a CEO, with or without loka sangraha.'** Everyone may not want to be the CEO of a company, but they still need to be the leader

of their life. They need to be successful at managing their goals and taking care of their parents, children, friends, or colleagues. They can practise the key lessons of Karm Yoga to refine their outlook and thought process in order to lead a balanced and successful life.

Work Quotient Qualities Nurtured by Lesson 5

- Community focus
- Visionary mindset
- Courage

> ### KEY TAKEAWAYS
>
> - One must choose to work in the spirit of loka sangraha.
> - The interconnected nature of today's world requires elevated thinking.
> - One must be careful when choosing one's role models.
> - One must learn how to balance community, individual, and business needs.
> - With loka sangraha, one can become a change-maker, a thought leader, and a visionary.

9

Karm Yoga Leadership Lesson 6: Do Not Work Only for the Fruits of the Action

Abhokta or the Non-Enjoyer Mindset

Inspiration exists, but it has to find you working.

—Pablo Picasso

The sixth Karm Yoga Leadership Lesson is that one must not work merely for the fruits of one's actions. This is explained in many shlokas of the Gita; notable among them are the following two:

karmanyevaadhikaaraste ma phaleshu kadaachana
ma karmaphala hetur bhurma sangostv akarmani

(Bhagavad Gita 2:47)

That is, you have the right to do the work but you do not have the right to its fruit. You should not think you are the cause of the result of the actions, or be attached to inaction.

mayi sarvaani karmaani sanyasyaadhyamta chetasa
nirashir nirmamo bhutva yudhyasva vigata jwarah

(Bhagavad Gita 3:30)

That is, be situated in yoga and perform your duty; do not worry about success or failure. Work with a *nirashir* attitude, or without expectations, and leave behind the desire for the fruits of the action.

One must honour one's work as a form of yoga and yagya by dedicating it to a higher power, and without worrying about the results. This refers to the acceptance of the fact that He is the owner and creator of the world. He is the final recipient of all efforts, so they should be performed in a manner that pleases Him—with excellence. This makes Karm Yoga akin to serving Him and the world.

This timeless philosophy inspires one to offer one's very best at every stage. Who would want to offer substandard work to the one they worship and/or respect? For instance, when a report has to be submitted to the CEO or the general manager, does the team not go the extra mile to ensure it is perfect? Now, imagine a position much higher than that. In that case, shouldn't one ensure the work is of the highest quality?

This mindset of excellence and dedication to the duty received from a higher power, after discarding the worry of the end result, can achieve tremendous results. It can be observed in the mindset of the Tokyo 2020 Summer Olympics gold medallist and the Paris 2024 Summer Olympics silver medallist javelin thrower Neeraj Chopra, who once said, 'Anytime I'm about to compete, I give it my absolute 100 per cent so that later I have no regrets about not doing everything I could have in that moment. I don't focus on the distance as much. I just focus on doing my best.'[23]

---

[23] 'Gold Standard: Neeraj Chopra and Abhinav Bindra', *India Today*, 25 October 2021, https://tinyurl.com/47c5ryks. Accessed on 31 May 2024.

This mindset allowed him to perform independently without tying himself to the result, and to discard doubt or constant worry, which can affect the quality of performance and diminish the possibility of success. The outcome: a simple farmer's son became the first Indian to win a gold medal in track and field at the Tokyo 2020 Summer Olympics.

Working in Nishkaam Karm Yoga

This process of engaging with purpose but without the desire of the result is called nishkaam Karm Yoga.

Not working for a result does not mean that one should be made to perform without remuneration, as has been misinterpreted often enough. It means that one should not get distracted by the thoughts of what one will earn, or what the outcome will be, or worry about future challenges. Instead, one should focus on the act alone with an abhokta or non-enjoyer mindset. This will free one from a distorted outlook, which can restrict growth and hamper one's chances of success. It will empower the individual to give up the fear, stress, ego, desire, and pride attached to the duty, but not the duty itself.

However, if one misunderstands the philosophy and gives up one's duty by wrongly choosing the renounced order of life, it will have an adverse impact on society. *Sanyasa* or renunciation is not uniformly prescribed, and definitely not to the untrained mind. Moreover, by simply stopping work, or refusing to perform it, no one can advance in life. It merely signifies that one is choosing renunciation as a means of running away from the challenges of the world. As a householder, one has to perform duties that include taking care of loved ones, ensuring their financial stability, and so on. Avoiding these will increase the lower gunas of rajo-guna and tamo-guna, and reduce the higher sattva-guna. Instead, one should learn to navigate and overcome the impact of the gunas with Karm Yoga.

sannyasah karm yogash cha nihshreya karaavubhau
tayostu karmsanyasaat karm yogo vishishyate

(Bhagavad Gita 5:2)

That is, action in Karm Yoga is better in comparison to the renunciation of work.

Thus, working without the expectation of the fruit is not an excuse to avoid duty; neither should it be avoided due to arrogance, fear, or pride (a rajo-guni action), nor should it be avoided out of lethargy (a tamo-guni action).

So one should continue to work without expectations, but does that mean one should not care for one's work? No, one can and must care for the work, without becoming attached to it. Attachment comes with emotional turmoil, which has no business in business anyway—after all, how can worry, fear, stress, anxiety, or dread help in the workplace?

Thus, Karm Yoga seeks to liberate the mind and work from desire-driven attachment by prioritizing duties, especially those that include a responsibility to others. They are accorded precedence over rites, rituals, and ceremonies.

From Karm to Nishkaam Karm: Work as a Liberating Force

The process of becoming nishkaam is a long journey, as performing all duties with an abhokta attitude is difficult. Let's understand why.

What is the common mindset towards work? 'I am the doer and I should get a great reward for it.' When an individual thinks along these lines (which is true for most workers and aspiring leaders), they may strive day and night to accomplish their goals. They may be inspired by the lure of an attractive salary, fame, recognition, a big bonus, or a promotion. The real/imaginary rewards and challenges ensure they are anxious even when they are with their loved ones. They may not mind cheating their colleagues to succeed and will be desperate for success, wanting it immediately. Or they may use work to avoid reality and the day-to-day responsibilities of life—like workaholics do, for example. Their overburdened state is a badge of honour for them. Such people are unable to enjoy work or life, rather they suffer due to their over-attachment to both.

Is this approach not common?

But now that you are aware of the teachings of Karm Yoga, the next time a challenge comes along, will you stop worrying? Will you stop working with anger, ego, and stress? Will you stop thinking only for yourself and start caring for your colleagues, family members, and the community? Will you stop competing with others just by reading about the Karm Yoga Lessons? Will you start taking care of the gunas and your mental health on day one?

Probably not. On the first day, it will be difficult. The

mind will react in the way that it is used to. It will make you dislike your colleague, make you annoyed at a loved one, increase your stress level, and fuel anger over a mistake. But you will at least be aware of what is happening, as you will have learnt to observe the self. This will make you aware of your mistakes, which is a good start on the noble path of Karm Yoga.

On the second or third day, you may try to control the mind. You will not snap at the intern or the colleague who needs your help. On the fourth or fifth day, you may be tempted by selfish desire to, say, steal a colleague's idea, and you may even give in. But with introspection, you will realize that ego has derailed you, and you will promise yourself to not do it the next time.

When your workload increases, you will counsel yourself to reduce the desire for self-indulgence (or at least, postpone it), and focus on discharging the duty. The next week, you may motivate a colleague to do the same. On some days, you will offer a prayer of gratitude for your duty; on other days (as you advance), you may be inspired to offer a prayer of well-being for the whole team/organization. In this way, if and when you try to improve regularly, all the small actions will add up and become a set of habits. After a few weeks or months, you will be able to enhance your mindset.

Yes, it will take time. It is arduous to change the self—arduous, but not impossible. It can be accomplished with the practice of the Karm Yoga Leadership Lessons at the workplace and at home, while nurturing the Work Quotient. These lessons will inspire you to perform your duty for the honour and joy of doing it. They will inspire you to enjoy each task, and the process of performing it.

Of course, it is difficult to not desire the fruits of the action, but can one at least begin to reduce the attachment to the worry associated with them? This is possible by performing with an abhokta or non-enjoyer mindset and offering gratitude on the action's completion, but not obsessing over its fate. Going ahead, you may adopt practices like a structured morning routine, self-care, introspecting about your purpose, staying calm, and so on. These will help you feel in control of yourself; you will become the one managing the day and the duty, and not vice versa. Duty with the right attitude is akin to meditation, and is the way to practise Karm Yoga.

Otherwise, the duty and your attachment to it will control and confine you to the restrictive label you may have given yourself, in terms of your role, background, identity, name, education, etc. These labels will distort your mindset, become a source of sorrow, anxiety, and stress, and set you up for failure.

Working with Freedom: A Personal Example

Many of us like to think of ourselves in terms of the work we do. But when faced with a challenge, we question the identity we have given ourselves. We ask ourselves: if we are not writers, doctors, businessmen, teachers, artists, journalists, or bloggers, then who are we?

Last year, I was working on a few poems but could not finish them, courtesy of a huge writer's block. It led me to wonder: what if I was not a writer or a poet? I was worried I would not be able to write and that readers would not appreciate my work, although I had barely begun. The worry about this imagined result hampered my creativity and led me to lose focus.

The label of a writer was one I had given myself; it was important for me to validate it, and that was not erroneous. But limiting myself to that identity, to the point that it became debilitating and evoked sorrow, fear, worry, and attachment, was erroneous. My fears should not have affected the work or me to such a large extent, and neither should the work have affected my mood. Both should have been independent and stable. However, that can only happen when the mind is liberated.

So when my stress level started rising, I realized my thought process was on the wrong track. I accepted that facing challenges, setbacks, or potential failure had made me doubt myself. But a stumbling block should not have engendered an identity crisis. It was my wrong thinking and excessive desires ('the poems should be completed quickly', 'the readers should like them', and so on) that were troubling me, not the world or anyone else. They confined me to one role alone and bound me to the work, making it difficult to enjoy either work or life.

These desires also made me overlook my other roles, those of a daughter, parent, sister, wife, neighbour, friend, devotee, daughter-in-law, and citizen. These roles were equally important and should have steadied me, but my limited thought process attached a label to the self and the work. It made me forget, albeit temporarily, to enjoy those roles and duties.

I also forgot that my duty was to write; the rest was out of my hands. Since I could not control anything or anybody beyond it, would worrying about it not restrict the unlimited self?

When we don't think along these lines and do not understand ourselves, we face an identity crisis or a mid-life crisis, if it happens at a certain age. Nowadays, even quarter-life crises and pre-mid-life crises have become common. With so many crises going on, we don't realize that the main one is that we have forgotten our true potential and inherent talent, and lost our courage and confidence. We are searching for shortcuts and avenues to avoid work or work less, but who are we really cheating?

This distressing struggle with our duty and ourselves gives rise to complex emotions—which is natural, but not managing them and becoming a victim to them is not. In times of crisis, we must renew our faith and keep our focus on the work, which is what I attempted to do. We must not measure our achievements, talent, potential, or strength by narrow materialistic standards and the expectations of others.

We need to enjoy our work and, at the same time, perform and enjoy our other roles as well. But is this common in the corporate world?

When Parag Agrawal, ex-CEO of X (formerly Twitter), an American microblogging and social-networking website, availed paternity leave after the birth of his second son, it became a big talking point on, well, X. Although it was the right thing to do, it was not a common practice among male workers, especially not at the CEO level.

This brings up many questions: Was he only a CEO, the label given to him by his organization? Was that his only role? Wasn't he also a father, a husband, a brother, a family person, and a son? Should he not have cared for his newborn child—after all, isn't fulfilling the familial duty as important as discharging the occupational one?

A leader prioritizing their personal or family needs over those of the business, even for a short time, should not be newsworthy anymore. Fathers actively raising their children is an idea that needs to be normalized for a more realistic and meaningful approach to work–life balance.

Whether an individual is a CEO, a homemaker, a writer, or a businessperson, if they are unable to step away from the duty for a few days or weeks, then it probably means that they are overly attached to it. This will not allow them to embrace all aspects of their lives, perform all their roles, or enjoy all the joys life has to offer, whether at home, in the workplace, or in the community.

We must not forget that we are not just the designation or pay cheque we receive, the manager we report to, or the expensive clothes and gadgets we buy; we are in essence the atma or soul, which is pure, eternal, and without labels.

indriyaani paraanyaahur indriyebhyah param manah
manasastu para buddhir yo buddheh paratastu sah

(Bhagavad Gita 3:42)

That is, our soul is the only thing infinite and constant in the world. The mind, intelligence, the organs, and ego are all lower than it.

After all, we are not merely economic beings, we are emotional, cultural, social, and spiritual beings who must work and live as responsible parts of the big picture; not with harmful ambition or unethical desires, but with gratitude, empathy, mindfulness, and love. We are potential karm yogis in action, ready to excel in our roles in meaningful and sustainable ways.

We deserve a work-life that is a source of liberation, and not a cause of attachment or sorrow.

The Akarm Concept: Action vs Inaction

Going ahead, as we strive to excel without focussing on results, we need to ensure we witness action and inaction on the same plane. This is the process of being an *akarm* worker, one with a spiritual attitude and a refined state of mind. It does not refer to a lack of duty or being inactive. If an individual is inactive, does that make them an akarm worker? No, they are being tamsik. When a tamo-guni person avoids action due to laziness, or when a rajo-guni person does so because it is difficult, they both get tied to the action. This means that they are affected due to their wrong attitude and will suffer the consequences of the abdication of duty.

Similarly, if a worker is engaged in a sattva-guni action, but expects a reward or benefit in return, their work will bind them. This is not what being an akarm worker means.

karmanyakarma yah pashyed akarmani cha karma yah
sa buddhimaan manushyeshu sa yuktah kritsna karm krit

(Bhagavad Gita 4:18)

That is, if one sees akarm in one's act, and witnesses karm in inaction, one can be considered intelligent and yogic in nature—such an individual is situated in yoga and is a true akarm worker. It is symbolic of their non-attached and non-doer state of mind.

Such an individual has accomplished all they can, does not need to achieve anything, and does not need to prove themselves to anyone. They may still be engaged in duty, but that is by choice. They are not bound by it; they are free and a leader at heart. This is one of the highest mindsets in Karm Yoga. It signifies that they are ready to continue irrespective of the result or the work. They have rejected the false restrictions of the world, its narrow labels, and the unevolved mindset that can shackle the unlimited self.

So even if they engage in, say, violence, they may not be bound by it. This is possible if they are an akarm worker. For example, a soldier is considered a karm yogi and not a murderer, as it is their duty to take part in war. It is their occupation that drives them, not a selfish objective. When they fight for their leader on the battlefield, they are not engaging in a wrongful action, so they are not bound by it.

yagyaarthaat karmanonyatralokoyam karm bandhanah
tadartham karm kaunteya mukta sangah samachar

(Bhagavad Gita 3:9)

That is, when one performs the duty as a sacrifice or dedicates it to a higher power, one escapes its binding effect.

Similarly, one is not bound when one stands up for the truth, protects one's loved ones or organization, prevents harm to or supports the oppressed, and works for the greater good. These acts are considered a service to the people, and thus a service unto Him.

How to Become an Akarm Worker: Work that Elevates

It is true that it is easy for a layperson of any gender (compared to a yogi) to get bound by their work. Even if they claim they do not desire anything, they may still be controlled by their thoughts and actions. For instance, mentally they may be thinking about enjoying a new product, or about the next venture they want to invest in. They may temporarily pause their actions, but the sense organs may be under the influence of their old habits. That is not being akarm. The Isha Upanishad explains in its second mantra how one can be an akarm worker:

*kurvanneveh karmaani jijeevisheshchchtam samaah
evam twayi naanythetosti na karm lipyate nare*

That is, one should work for a hundred years or till death; it is the right way to work. Work will bind, but one can utilize the pure knowledge to set the self free. Even when work does bind, it should still be performed if it can help another. This is not considered wrong and is a pure form of karm and dharma.

Thus, it is clear that practising dharma along with action offers maximum benefit. Such a mindset is nirashir (mentioned earlier in Bhagavad Gita 3:30), and 'burns' all the reactions of an individual's work, both good and bad. That is, they become unaffected by its binding nature to find peace, joy, and success.

Adopting the Nishkaam and Abhokta Attitude

An individual can practise the nishkaam mindset by:

- enhancing spiritual knowledge and the knowledge of Karm Yoga to refine their thought process;
- reducing their selfish desires, and if they do come to the fore, avoiding acting on them;
- increasing the dharmic desires that are necessary for the householder stage of life;
- performing the duties in a detached way, not thinking of themselves as the doer or expecting good results;
- performing with devotion, knowledge, and action;
- viewing action and inaction on the same plane;
- being confident in their abilities and thinking independently: 'Even if others do not reciprocate my goodwill or do not support me, I am unaffected as I do not depend on them for validation or motivation';
- supporting the family and team members, even when they cannot offer them help in return; and
- working with discipline and gratitude. They must not be bored or cynical, but genuinely enjoy performing their responsibilities (while reducing multitasking).

Working in this way, a yogi can attain freedom or *mukti*. What does mukti symbolize here? It symbolizes the mukti on earth, one that the karm yogic life offers, which ensures the individual is free from stress, sorrow, anxiety, ego, and a flawed attitude towards work. It allows them to rise above the challenges of the world and the ignorance of the self: it is self-empowerment and self-realization at its finest.

Addressing Some Common Arguments and Doubts

- **'Either a higher power does not exist, or I don't know how to find inspiration in Him. So how can I dedicate my work to Him?'** A common Indian saying goes that if anyone tries hard enough, they can find anything; so why not Him? One needs to find Him within. But even if one cannot, one need not worry about His existence. If one does find Him, that is wonderful, but if one does not, that is great too. Tattva Bodha can help one understand that the entire creation is pervaded by the higher truth, and that can be one's source of inspiration to live and work better.
- **'I don't believe in multiple lives or rebirth, so I do not want to be nishkaam.'** If one does not believe in this concept, one can choose to believe in science. It is a fact that energy can neither be created nor destroyed, but can be transformed. So, one can consider the self a pure form of energy. It has always existed, it exists today, and will continue to exist in the future.

Work Quotient Qualities Nurtured by Lesson 6

- A winning attitude
- Determination and confidence
- Equanimity

KEY TAKEAWAYS

- Perform like the divine, with a liberated and nishkaam attitude.
- If practising the nishkaam attitude is not possible, engage with a sakaam attitude.
- Prevent the harmful effect of work, don't stop performing the duty.
- Action will not bind when performed with an akarm spirit.
- The self is not merely an economic being, but also an emotional, a cultural, a social, and a spiritual being.

10

Karm Yoga Leadership Lesson 7: Surrender the Ego, Do Not Think You Are the Doer

Akarta or the Non-Doer Mindset

maya taje toh kya hua, maan taja na jaye,
maan bade muniwar gaye, maan saban ko khaye.

[It is easier to give up wealth than the ego.
Ego troubles even great people.]

—Kabir

The seventh and final Karm Yoga Leadership Lesson is to surrender the ego, and reject the label of the doer. Karm Yoga lays great stress on the renunciation of the *ahamkara* or the false ego, rather than merely renouncing material possessions. Thus, the one who successfully reduces the ego is considered more advanced than any other yogi. But this has to be accomplished while the individual is engaged in worldly duties; to not perform one's duty is considered to be against one's nature and the principles of the world. One has to perform them all till the last breath, without ego, the only caveat being that the duties should lead to common good, or at least should not harm anyone. This does not imply giving up on the quality of the duty, or the time or effort invested in it, only the false pride binding one to it.

Problems Caused by an Ego-Driven Mindset

Why does Karm Yoga encourage abandoning pride? Because the ego creates numerous problems for the self. It covers the intellect like a layer of dust that is difficult to clear and ties one to desires, bad habits, sorrow, anger, and finally failure. It makes one desire unending wealth and power, while making one avoid spiritual responsibilities or a higher purpose.

*prakriteh kriyamaanaani gunaih karmaani sarvashah
ahankaara vimudhatma kartaaham iti manyate*

(Bhagavad Gita 3:27)

That is, the one with false ego believes they are the doer of activities.

A person with such a mindset believes, 'Everybody apart from me is responsible for my challenges and failures.' It leads to intense attachment with the work, role, status, and wealth. It makes them take credit for the team's success, making them believe that they are better than others. But in times of failure, they may prefer to blame luck, destiny, family, other team members, the COO, the world, and even the Higher Power. The more attached and ignorant they are, the greater their fears become. They live in constant worry and anxiety about what will happen in the future.

A Role Model to Look Up to: The Best Karm Yogi

How can this harmful ego be reduced? With the support of the Higher Power, who is the Yogeshwar or the god of yoga, the first and the most accomplished yogi. Lord Shiva, known as the Yogeshwar,

- performs in the spirit of Karm Yoga;
- approaches duty with joy and excellence—His creations are perfect, just like His work;
- works with pure knowledge, which leads to exceptional results;
- does not work with anger, fear, doubt, etc.;
- does not stop engaging with His duties if they are tough or tedious; and
- does not get attached to the task or its result.

Thus, He is the ultimate *prerak* or inspiration, the best karm and gyan yogi (being the incarnation of knowledge itself), who inspires one to work with excellence.

na me paarthaasti kartavyam trishu lokeshu kinchana
naanavaaptam avaaptavyam varta eva cha karmani

(Bhagavad Gita 3:22)

In the above shloka, Lord Krishna explained how there was no work assigned to Him in the three planets, He did not require anything, but He still performed all His duties.

Thus, even though He does not seek (or want) fame or wealth, He strives day and night to support every being because He does not want to set a wrong example. If He stops discharging his duties, the common people will do the same. So, He continues with a nishkaam attitude and inspires everyone to become the *prerit karta* or the inspired worker.

How can this help?

The *sharnagati* or spirit of surrender can free the aspiring leader (the prerit) to think creatively, collaborate effectively, and lead boldly with a nishkaam attitude.

*sarva dharmaan parityajya mam ekam sharanam vraja
aham tvaam sarva paapebhyo mokshayishyaami ma shuchah*

(Bhagavad Gita 18:66)

That is, leave everything else and surrender to Him, and He will protect you from all sins.

It is akin to seeking the refuge of pure knowledge to remove doubt and fear, so one can live and work with purpose and clarity. But if He is the owner of everything (and all work), how can one surrender what one doesn't own? By giving up the false ego that makes one believe one is the doer and is driving the world. This reduces the feeling of ownership, selfishness, and attachment. The thought process is transformed: 'Even if something unfortunate happened, so what? It cannot defeat or define me.' One stops wondering or complaining about the different incidents in life and takes them in one's stride.

Bold enough to live by their convictions, such a person does not wait for the approval of others to forge ahead. Instead, they understand others' limiting fears and offer support, so they too can evolve with them. Free from their weaknesses and the tag of the doer, they are truly liberated as an akarta or non-doer.

To understand this evolved state, we need to look no further than the life of Rani Lakshmi Bai, the Indian queen of the state of Jhansi from 1843 to 1858. After King Gangadhar Rao passed away, she stood up to the East India Company and refused to hand over her kingdom (Lesson 6: action without the fear of the results). She became one of the key leaders of the Indian Rebellion of 1857 and fought bravely for her people (Lesson 5: loka sangraha). She died in battle but energized the independence struggle through her dynamism and resilience (Lesson 7: akarta attitude). An ego-less leader who practised Karm Yoga, her heroic tales continue to inspire the nation even today.

Handling the Dual Nature of the World

As seen in the example above, the akarta attitude in the practice of Karm Yoga can help one navigate the many challenges of life. These challenges usually present themselves in pairs: success–failure, joy–sorrow, wealth–poverty, *raag–dwesh* (attachment–hatred), heat–cold, and so on.

sukha dukhe same kritvaa laabhalaabhau jayaajayau
tato yuddhyaay yujyasva naivam paapam avaapsyasi

(Bhagavad Gita 2:38)

That is, one has to perform the duty without considering joy or sorrow, loss or gain, victory or defeat, as they will always exist in some form or another.

Success–Failure

When success comes, one has to handle it gently, as sometimes it is tougher than handling failure.

Hasn't one heard of movie stars and famous artists who could not cope with their overnight success and public adulation? They fell into the trap of addiction or suffered from depression due to various factors. Some realized after achieving global fame and massive wealth that these were not all that they had hoped for, and did not offer them the joy or stability they needed.

To manage success, one must approach it in the following ways:

- The credit for success must be shared with the entire team and loved ones.
- It must be accepted with gratitude towards Him.
- It must not inflate the ego and make one belittle others.
- One must not be 'over the moon' after achieving a milestone.
- One must share the success/wealth with those who are less fortunate.
- One must practise meditation to calm the mind.
- One must continue working hard and not rest on one's past laurels.

Similarly, if one fails, one must not be crushed, or lose confidence. Rather, one must:

- undertake the responsibility for failure, which can occur due to many factors, including the unfolding of the *prarabdh karm*, or the sum of past actions bearing fruit in the present life;
- analyse its cause, take time to regroup, and bounce back;
- motivate the family or team and support them during this time;

- remain resilient on the path of Karm Yoga, never giving up on one's dreams;
- restart the same or a different project with renewed vigour and drive; and
- face all challenges with a mature attitude, and without doubt or loss of courage.

When facing either success–failure or glory–infamy, one must remain slightly detached. These should not defeat or conquer one; instead one must accept them with grace, good humour, patience, and humility.

*yam hi na vyathayantyete purusham purusharshabha
sama duhkhah sukham dhiram so mritatvaaya kalpate*

(Bhagavad Gita 2:15)

That is, only the one who is *dhir*, or not disturbed by happiness or sorrow, is eligible for liberation.

Wealth–Poverty

The same holds true for managing one's attitude towards excessive wealth or the lack of it. Indeed, poverty is a serious global issue, and was referred to as the biggest sorrow by the renowned Indian saint Tulsidas.

However, this does not mean that the biggest joy in the world is extreme wealth. Both are considered destabilizing in Karm Yoga; both the absence and excess of wealth drive one to commit wrong acts, either when acquiring it or when trying to retain or increase it by hook or crook. The ancient sages observed that even if one acquired all the gold, success, and fame along with all the desirable men or women in the world, one would still not be satisfied.

Nowadays there are many other forms of acquisition, like bitcoins, non-fungible tokens (NFT; a non-interchangeable unit of data that is stored on a blockchain), investing in the metaverse, and so on. Yes, the financial success they represent is key to supporting the aspirations of the self and the family. But they must be used to meet ethical needs and not as a means of hoarding wealth, or they will become a source of challenges in the future—a tidal wave of unending desires that can never be satisfied.

To prevent this, one must genuinely believe that the resources of the world have not been created for one's personal use, but are for everyone. Only then can one grow into a responsible and socially conscious person, and finally into a yogi.

Raag–Dwesh

One cannot perform to the best of one's abilities if controlled by raag or dwesh. Be it in the stock market, in the boardroom, or at home, the individual stands to lose each time they let their emotions get the better of them.

Both extreme attachment and hatred can set one up for problems. One may mistakenly believe that raag is better than dwesh, as it denotes affection, but both are different sides of the same coin and contain an element of ownership and ego. Just like any other powerful emotion, they destabilize the mind, and make one either too attached or too intolerant of a loved one or team member, or a thing or process.

In the workplace, for example, a manager filled with these unbalanced emotions will upset the equilibrium of the team.

They will be annoyed to see a worker they do not like and pleased to see the one they prefer. The quality of their work will fluctuate depending on their mood.

At home, they may be overcome with rage or jealousy towards a relative whom they perceive as a threat. Sometimes, they may not even realize why their behaviour has changed. It is only after the emotions overpower their better judgement that they may realize their impact.

Raag–dwesh may be natural, but living a life of distraction and performing one's duty under their control is not. One can stabilize the self with the akarta attitude, and enhance one's Work Quotient through Karm Yoga.

Implementing the Akarta Mindset: Work Is Its Own Reward

Who can benefit from managing the dual nature of the world with an akarta attitude? Anyone and everyone can benefit from it. One need not be a CEO, general manager, or homemaker. No matter where one is or what one's current position is, one can decide to start advancing. There is no special timeline, qualification, or calendar required to evolve into a better person, householder, worker, leader, or team player. Only the inner awakening is necessary to begin; and perseverance is required to advance on this chosen path.

The only exception is that one engaged in adharmic acts cannot claim, 'I am ego-less, I am nishkaam.' Even if they are performing these acts for someone else, if they are exploiting another, cheating, or engaging in violence when it isn't part of their duty/swadharma (as it is for soldiers), they cannot be considered an akarta. Remember, those acts are performed with buddhi and not with Buddhi Yoga, as explained in Leadership Lesson 2. Similarly, a person who is arrogantly engaging in rajo-guni actions, not for themselves but for their organization, cannot claim to be an akarta either. Instead, they must do the following:

- They must accept their spiritual essence—the real, higher Self, which is stable, joyful, and complete—and realize that it is the ego that is dissatisfied, angry, and desperate.
- They must introspect and master the gunas and their behaviour, drivers, strengths, and weaknesses, and manage the emotions that overpower them, like anger, greed, lust, wrath, etc. (as explained in Chapter 1).
- They must not be unaffected or uncaring; that is not what it means to be an akarta. But they must be able to put their emotions aside with a single-minded focus on the goal. The ability to tolerate and restrain the self and maintain a viveki attitude signals maturity and strength in the journey towards success with Karm Yoga.
- They should empower the body, as it is an instrument of action, knowledge, and liberation. As per ancient Indian philosophy, all other *loka*s or worlds, like *swarga loka* or heaven and *narak loka* or hell, were created to either savour or suffer the results of actions, while only *karm loka* or the Earth was designed to allow the human body to perform the duty.
- Even when engaged in duty, they must believe that they are not the doer. That is, they are independent of the work and its effect, as they are a prerit karta.

- They must perform the duty for honour and joy, regardless of the wealth or glory it may bring.
- They must challenge themselves in order to gauge their potential and that of the family or team. A small goal is easily achievable, so it will not be inspiring enough to move someone out of their comfort zone.

There may be problems resulting due to a job. If one is employed in a job, one may be preventing another from getting employed in it; if one is selling a product, one may be preventing another from selling something similar. One must not abandon the duty simply for these reasons.

With an akarta mindset, one can become a game changer who sets new benchmarks of behaviour and excellence with action and thought leadership. It will free the self from the binding nature of work and grant one the sublime blessing of pure success. It will eventually bring one to the higher realization, 'I am the akarta and *avyaya*—I am not the doer and I am infinite':

vedaavinaashinam nityam ya enam ajam avyayam

(Bhagavad Gita 2:21)

The Journey Beyond: Work as Destiny

After achieving material goals such as wealth, fame, success, and the like, a common question that emerges is whether one should give up work; that is, retire and step back from active participation in life and from the business world.

There are different schools of thought regarding this. Some philosophers believe that after one has mastered Karm

Yoga, one can move on to the next stage of growth called Gyan Yoga, the art of knowledge. It requires a contemplative and introverted mindset initially. But one cannot skip Karm Yoga and head directly to it; one's growth needs to be sequential for it to be beneficial. Only after one's mind is ready to accept knowledge in Gyan Yoga can one transition to a higher consciousness.

It is not important for the *gyani* to work, but they can still perform duties, if required or by choice. This is based on the example of divinity. The ancient sages explained that despite being a *param gyani* (ultimate source of knowledge), He was engaged in both Karm and Gyan Yoga. He discharged all the duties even when He did not need to. If He could, why can't the rest of us? The sages believed that one could acquire knowledge and continue with one's responsibilities, that is, be both a gyani and a karm yogi.

On the other hand, there were some philosophers who believed that one could be in the working stage throughout life, if necessary. Progress could not be hurried, and those who were not ready for advancement could continue to improve within a particular stage, as it required many years, and sometimes many births, to advance. It was not necessary for them to retire if they were in a position to contribute to society; they could continue to function as karm yogis for life.

However, some believed that work could not do more than purify the mind, and once the practice of Karm Yoga had been perfected, the mind would become free from the untruths of the world and ready to absorb the knowledge of Gyan Yoga.

As per the Gita, though, both the Sankhya Yoga of the gyanis and the Karm Yoga of the karm yogis eventually led to *param siddhi* or empowerment.

*yat saankhyaih praapyate sthaanam tad yogair api gamyate
ekam saankhyam cha yogam, cha yah pashyati sa pashyati*

(Bhagavad Gita 5:5)

That is, the art of knowledge and the art of action are not contradictory in nature, rather they lead to the same goal. They may be different routes, but action is not below knowledge in stature. Both do not require any tools or gadgets to practise them. They require a committed mind, a disciplined approach, and constant practice to ensure progress.

This makes it clear that it is not necessary to give up the duty in any stage of life, whether as an aspiring karm yogi or gyan yogi, or a combination of both. In this way, the ancient Indian philosophers offered different alternatives to manage work-life, depending on the personality and outlook of the person. But they highlighted the importance of duty for every path, in order to ensure no one would be misled or abandon it for any reason.

This completes the 7 Lessons of Karm Yoga: when one performs with a nishkaam, abhokta mindset and as an akarta who discharges the swadharma with Buddhi, Bhakti, and Gyan Yoga in the spirit of loka sangraha, one will be ensured financial and spiritual success in this life and the next.

Addressing Some Common Arguments and Doubts

- **'Practising Karm Yoga and/or being an akarta is for saints.'** Karm Yoga is specifically designed for householders and those who have completed the first stage of life, that is brahmacharya or student life. It, along with Bhakti Yoga, is applicable and relevant to everyone. Being an akarta needs the right attitude, not a lifestyle of renunciation. A householder with a reduced ego is considered equal to a yogi and an akarta when they perform their duties with integrity.

- **'How will Karm Yoga help me detach?' or 'I do not want to be detached.'** In modern times, detachment does not mean that a worker or householder should not care about their loved ones, other people, or things. It means they should detach from ignorance, stress, unhealthy thought patterns, and toxic habits. They must ensure a good distance from the selfish desires that can harm them, and actively seek to remove them. They must then attach themselves to work, to a purpose, to knowledge, to their higher nature, and to a controlled ego.

Work Quotient Qualities Nurtured by Lesson 7

- Controlling the ego
- Resilience
- Joyfulness

KEY TAKEAWAYS

- Do not consider yourself as the doer.
- You can become an akarta with sharnagati, practice, and detachment.
- The ego needs to be reduced in order for an individual to reach their potential.
- The akarta mindset allows one to be liberated.
- An akarta continues learning and growing throughout their life.

Conclusion

Karm Yoga in Action: Eternal Philosophy for the New Age

Arise, awake and stop not till the goal is reached.

—Swami Vivekananda

The philosophy of Karm Yoga and its 7 Lessons is both a journey and destination with one key condition to begin with: that one must perform the duty. It does not matter where, when, or why the duty is performed, what the nature of the task is, what type of process it is, or what the location or identity of the doer is. Its successful implementation depends on one's readiness, experience, attitude, and capacity.

No one can force another to adopt the path of Karm Yoga. The inspiration to embark on it must come from within, and once that happens, one can enthusiastically advance on this thought-provoking magical journey. It will help one live and work like a leader, reach one's full potential, and achieve the extraordinary.

It is challenging, no doubt, as it requires sacrifice, discipline, and refusing temporary pleasure for future gain, but it does get easier with practice. On the other hand, its alternative is a life of insecurity, anxiety, anger, sorrow, and uncontrollable desires.

How to Implement Karm Yoga in Life

As one aspiring for success, you can perform the following steps to practise Karm Yoga:

- **Improve your awareness of the teachings of Karm Yoga:** You can read literature and texts by great saints, intellectuals, and other inspirational leaders to enhance your knowledge of Karm Yoga in particular, and spirituality in general. Also, attend discussions, events, online classes, or lectures on related topics.
- **Seek the advice of a trusted source:** You can seek the support of a guru, a mentor, or an experienced professional to guide you in this journey. Supplement it by reading about the lives of leaders like Swami Vivekananda and Mahatma Gandhi, amongst others, as their lives showcase Karm Yoga in action.
- **Practise the 7 Lessons of Karm Yoga as best as you can:** If at any point during the practice you are unable to follow the principles, you can adjust your approach accordingly. It does not matter if you are at a lower or higher stage, what is important is to learn and grow with each lesson:
    - If you cannot become an akarta or non-doer, consider the self as the karta or doer of your own work, and do not steal or take credit for another's efforts. You must give due credit to the team and family for their contribution.
    - If you cannot think of yourself as an abhokta or non-enjoyer, and if you want to enjoy the fruits of your actions, at least share them with others.
    - If you cannot work in loka sangraha projects, work on

projects that do not expressly harm the community.
- If you cannot practise Buddhi Yoga, work with buddhi directed towards the accomplishment of ethical goals.
- If you cannot envisage work as worship, think of it as a responsibility that needs to be discharged.
- If you cannot increase good or dharmic activities, avoid engaging in adharmic ones that can harm others.
- If you cannot discharge all your responsibilities, focus on the key ones initially, then gradually learn to manage the rest of them.

- **Improve self-talk:** If you aspire to be a karm yogi, it is critical that you understand yourself, hone your strengths, and reduce your weaknesses. This cannot be accomplished if your mind is not under control. So, on a daily basis, motivate yourself to perform your duties with excellence and without expecting results. This has to be repeated every day till you don't need a reminder. Encourage yourself to be patient, positive, and focussed. Then, in real-world conversations, use the same language and behaviour to reinforce the message. Do not put yourself down or be harsh with the self; that is not humility, and it will only serve to deplete your confidence.
- **Make a Goals Journal:** A karm yogi is purpose-driven and goal-oriented, so you must aim to be too. You need to find your higher purpose or calling. This may take time, but it will come to you eventually. Use a Goals Journal to help in planning; enumerate your long-term goals that will help you fulfil your purpose, and the reason for each goal and its relative importance. Break them down into

smaller tasks that need to be performed on a daily basis. Ensure they are prioritized, and review the list every evening. Know which ones are pending and why; commit to a timeline to realize them. Remember, everyone has the same amount of time, so you must make the best of it. Add both spiritual and material goals for balance.
- **Ask what a karm yogi would do:** In a difficult situation, ask yourself how a yogi would behave, then react in the same way till it becomes a natural response. If a karm yogi fails, they do not lose faith and neither should you. If they succeed, they stay grounded and grateful, and so should you. Initially, it may be difficult to maintain equipoise, but keep at it with confidence and cheer.
- **Accept the possibility of loss/failure:** Your goals need to be supported by an action plan, as discussed earlier, but you must also keep a Plan B ready in case the first one does not succeed. Challenges, failures, and problems are facts of life, but instead of suffering at their hands, why not prepare for them? Encourage innovative thinking, reward risk-takers in the team, explore new markets, adopt digitalization, and anticipate the impact of artificial intelligence and its subsequent effect on customers, amongst other things, to cushion the impact of failure in business.
- **Ensure dama or physical discipline:** Unless you take care of your health, your goals will remain a distant dream (Chapter 2). Develop new habits and discard the old ones that don't align with your purpose. Inculcate habits that encourage daily discipline to support you in this quest: time management, an organized morning routine, exercise, sleep, hygiene, and a nutritious diet,

amongst others. Choose what works for you; some may be comfortable with yoga as a form of exercise, and others with jogging, Pilates, or weight training.

- **Ensure shama or mental discipline:** Bringing the mind under control is a daily practice in Karm Yoga. If you have self-doubt or suffer from mental turmoil, it needs to be managed with meditation, pranayama, chanting, and other methods. Seek the refuge of Bhakti Yoga and do not allow the mind to dwell on negativity. Increase your sattva-guna, and try to reduce the lower gunas (Chapter 1). You can also practise daily affirmations that are in line with your goals, or chant 'Om', the divine syllable, or specific statements to stabilize emotions.
- **Spend time with the right people:** If you surround yourself with people who are evolved thinkers, or maybe even aspiring karm yogis, you will make faster progress. Recruit or associate with inspiring colleagues, spend more time with innovative thinkers, and seek the company of like-minded professionals with whom you can collaborate.
- **React less, resist less (both online and offline):** Everything does not need a reaction, especially on social media. Witness both the good and bad in it and use it to serve you, not the other way round. If you must react or resist, resist spending more time in your comfort zone.
- **Instil stress management as a daily act:** Stress is an integral part of work-life, so accept its existence, but reduce its impact. Practise meditation, yoga, mudras, pranayama, prayer, etc., to reduce stress, increase sattva-guna, and nurture the viveki mindset.
- **Assess yourself:** At every stage, gauge whether you are

working in the spirit of Karm Yoga or not. Before beginning any big task, ask yourself the following questions:
- Have I nourished the self with positive thoughts, nutrition, and rest, in preparation of the responsibility? If not, will I do it tomorrow, or the next time I have a task?
- Will I accept my duty with gratitude?
- Will I perform it with a joyful attitude, leading to an elevated/better performance?
- Will I postpone the desire to indulge in order to focus on the task at hand?
- Will my self-confidence be shaken when I encounter a challenge?
- How will I avoid getting worked up before beginning the task?
- Will my mind be distracted and worry about the result?
- Is work a pleasure or pressure for me?

This small pause and habit of introspection will help you refresh your attitude, adjust your frame of mind, and address any foreseeable problem.

- **Nurture the required Work Quotient qualities:** These qualities elevate the thought process, sharpen the intellect, and re-engineer the attitude:
  - Lesson 1: Self-reliance, hard work, commitment, and a duty-oriented mindset
  - Lesson 2: Empathy, faith, and treating everyone equally
  - Lesson 3: Excellence, knowledge, focus, and balance
  - Lesson 4: Discipline and stability, integrity and

ethics, and innovation
- Lesson 5: Community focus, a visionary mindset, and courage
- Lesson 6: A winning attitude, confidence, and equanimity
- Lesson 7: Control of ego, resilience, and joyfulness

There may be others (depending on one's role and personality), but these cover the broad spectrum of qualities that are required to become successful in managing the self and others. Chapters 4–10 list the traits nurtured by the respective Karm Yoga Lessons.

- **Visualize your journey/growth and create success daily:** The very fact that you are attempting to evolve is a positive sign on this voyage. Imagine this—you are engaging with your duties with joy, for the sheer pleasure and honour of performing them. See yourself waking up refreshed and giving your 100 per cent to all your tasks. Your mood is stable, engaged, and cheerful. You complete your work regularly and achieve your short- and long-term goals. You help others in their journey and contribute to the community. Your work is an elevating, deeply satisfying, and transformative experience that leads to bliss, good health, and peace. Visualize this every day and reward yourself in order to stay on track.

How will you know if you are making progress and succeeding? You can align your mindset with that of a karm yogi's and compare or check whether you are on track.

A karm yogi sheds the baggage of unnecessary suffering,

stress, and sorrow of the past or worry of the future when engaged in their work. They function with higher intelligence and equanimity. This equanimity is yoga itself, and a key ingredient for every person who wants to master themselves. It does not include complacency or taking a back seat in life; it signifies being confident and balanced, based on one's swadharma and value system.

The karm yogi approaches their work with *nishtha*, which means they cannot be moved from their goal, and they persist even when it is difficult. This is called being *nishthavaan*. The one situated in knowledge is the *gyan nishth*, and the one situated in work is the *karm nishth*. Both are stable in nature and do not give up amidst challenging situations.

The karm yogi works for success but is not desperate for it; they are secure due to their faith and self-confidence. They have clear goals, but if these are not fulfilled, they are able to accept that and renew efforts to accomplish them in a different way. They believe that success doesn't lie in increasing the number of acquisitions for the office or home, but in how much they can give to or share with their team and loved ones. They work with a customer-centric approach and strive for innovative solutions. They develop a social consciousness and view the business as a meaningful part of the community. They accept the higher self as an abhokta, and work with this elevated attitude at home, at the office, and in the community.

The sum of these actions and behaviours is Karm Yoga, and when you start working and thinking like this, you will also be considered a karm yogi.

If you can ensure this level of personal change, there is

no reason why you will not be able to bring about change in your home, community, and workplace as well. This will lead to continuous, sustainable, and meaningful progress, which otherwise may not be possible with the 'business as usual' attitude.

The Past and the Future Converge with Karm Yoga

Individuals and businesses cannot and should not continue as usual in this era of disruption and geopolitical conflicts. It needs everyone to embrace change now.

Within change resides hope. We can no longer take the cautious route and wait for someone else to come along to implement the bold and much-needed initiatives. We have to do it ourselves. Many have struggled with the insecurity and uncertainty posed by the pandemic and its aftermath, as well as the many wars playing out in different corners of the world, but this cannot be an excuse for stagnation.

True, the economy and the world is in flux, but we need not be. The challenges of the world will continue, and so must we. Yesterday the challenge was the Covid-19 virus; tomorrow it will be some other threat.

As we have seen in the preceding chapters, the need of the hour is awareness and implementation of the profound philosophy of Karm Yoga. With it, those aspiring to be successful will be able to bring their attitude, value system, skills, and mindset under control. They can discard their myopic vision and shape their destiny in a changing world, although their essence is unchanging.

Going ahead, what will also remain the same are the

hands in which the power and responsibility to implement people-friendly policies is concentrated: the CEOs, industry titans, business gurus, and corporate philosophers. Didn't someone once say that with great power comes great responsibility? As such, these leaders should assume the responsibility to disrupt the existing dynamic, in which communities and businesses function as selfish, individualistic entities with profit as the overarching motive. They must create a new system that accelerates the sharing of power and resources, rethink and redefine their relationship with themselves and with their work and people, and listen to them with respect, so that all can be partners in this wondrous journey of growth. Together, they can adapt to the needs of the next normal, whenever it may come and however it may look. This will future-proof them and help them withstand any shocks that lie in store for them.

Indeed, the pandemic and the wars have affected the political, social, intellectual, and economic landscape of the world dramatically, in terms of technology, resources, digitalization, attitudes, and the site of performance of work. The evolved, borderless nature of the work of today needs open hearts and minds to match its metamorphosis. Each and every individual, from the top brass to the grassroots worker, must go all out to bring out the best in each other, while minimizing discrimination, inequity, and mistreatment, in order to navigate the post-pandemic, war-afflicted economy with flair and aplomb.

It is in the interest of the management to ensure that this happens, and it is good for the business, community, and individual too. They have nothing to lose except ego, greed, guilt, anger, worry, and regret, and a lot to gain in terms of a whole new world of opportunity with forward-thinking teams, innovation, digitalization, hybrid systems, and novel processes. If they attempt to achieve this goal with karmic faith and a small ego, it can be implemented successfully.

When the leaders and their organizations succeed in their efforts, they will create the base of a compassionate, fair, and responsible society that offers equal and meaningful opportunities, leading to harmony and prosperity. This will lead to a future where excellence will be the norm, creativity will be encouraged, and job satisfaction will be a given. The resulting workplaces will be flexible, humane, and nurturing, with a healthy work culture where every voice will matter, every contribution valued, and every individual aspiration met. All shareholders and stakeholders will have a bright future designed by them, and will be able to balance spiritual goals with material ones.

In such an organization, customers will be honoured with quality and seamless solutions across geographies. Its leaders will be sahishnu and jaishnu. Its teams will be agile, collaborative, inspired, and engaged. They will not seek to have it all, but to do it all, which in turn will help them achieve it all. They will be dharmic, viveki, sattvik, dedicated to swadharma, and will work with Buddhi Yoga, not mere buddhi.

When duty will be respected as worship, a skill in action, a sublime source of bliss, a form of art, an evolution of yoga and yagya, and the path to a higher consciousness, it will mark the successful integration of Karm Yoga into life.

This will empower the common person and the aspiring leader to engage with meaning, joy, peace, dignity, and commitment. They will be treated right, and function like an akarta, an abhokta, and a leader in loka sangraha. They will fulfil their potential and be the best version of themselves, and will find true success and prosperity in their heart and in the world. This will enable union with the self, and can serve as a gateway to the union with the higher Self, leading to self-realization.

As grateful seekers, we have wonderful things to accomplish, and much to learn, share, and contribute. In the promising future that awaits us, the sky is not the limit, nor is the quantum world or the multiverse. The only condition is that we should not stop evolving and emerging, caring and helping, sharing and seeking, and growing and advancing.

We can do all of that and so much more. Everything we want to be, we can be; everything we want to achieve, we can; everything we can potentially conceive of, we can accomplish. Everything we are seeking, we can and will discover. Whatever the goal, we will achieve it with the sacred magic of the energy fields, the wonder of the creative fields, and the power of the yogic fields in and around us. Together, we can do it.

Acknowledgements

I am very grateful for the support offered by my parents, late grandparents, parents-in-law, husband, son, and extended family at every stage of life; none of it would have been possible without your love and support.

To my grandfather, the late Vishnu Kant Shastri, gratitude for everything, really. He was a mentor, philosopher, and guide, and I truly felt his support during this journey. He used to seek the blessings of his guru Swami Akhandananda when he embarked on a new project, and I seek his blessings. Today and always.

His Divine Grace A.C. Bhaktivedanta Swami Prabhupada for blessing us and being a universal source of inspiration.

Thank you to my sister Vibha Batra, brother-in-law, and niece for their support.

Special thanks to my current and ex-colleagues, friends, acquaintances, and everyone else who shared their valuable inputs. I would like to thank Smitha Reddy and Sanjay Jupudi of Qentelli, Vivek Jalan of Talent Sharks, Rishal Sharma, Nupur Shrivastava, and Daniel Jebasingh of Covenant Consultants, Ajay Ganesh of SunEdison, Priya Vivek of Qoruz, Nitesh Kripalani, ex-country head and director at Amazon Video India, Vijaya Ghosh of Accenture, and so many others who spoke to me, some on and some off the record.

A big thanks to my publisher Rupa Publications and editor Dibakar Ghosh—your support means a lot to me. You guys always push me to give my best and, really, I can't thank you enough for having faith in me. Thank you to Kapish Mehra, MD, Rupa Publications, for having faith in my vision. And my heartfelt thanks to Gauri Chopra, assistant copy editor, for all the help in the edit process.

Finally, a big thank you to my readers—you encourage and inspire me everyday.